DAVE MATTHEWS BAND
Fan Favorites FOR DRUMS

T0087313

2 Crush

12 Dancing Nancies

23 Everyday

35 Grey Street

45 Jimi Thing

56 The Space Between

61 Tripping Billies

69 Two Step

80 Warehouse

92 Where Are You Going

99 *Drum Notation Legend*

Transcribed by Scott Schroedl

Cover photo by Danny Clinch

ISBN 1-57560-687-9

Cherry Lane Music Company

Director of Publications/Project Editor:
Mark Phillips

Manager of Publications:
Rebecca Quigley

Visit our website at www.cherrylane.com

CRUSH

Words and Music by
David J. Matthews

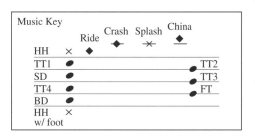

Intro

Moderately slow ♩ = 94

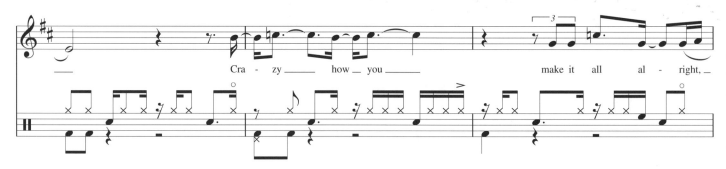

things _ you _ do. _____ And I _____ do _____ for _ you _____

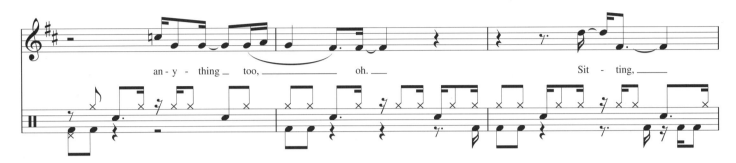

an - y - thing _ too, _____ oh. _____ Sit - ting, _____

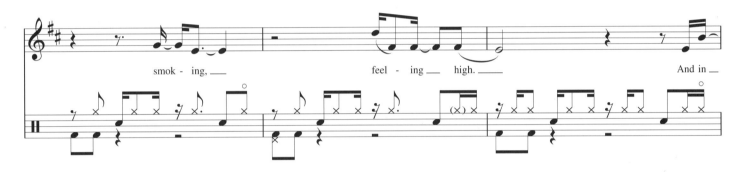

smok - ing, ___ feel - ing _ high. _____ And in _

____ this _____ mo - ment, _____ oh, it feels so right. _

Pre-Chorus

Love - ly la - dy, _____ I am at _____ your feet,

____ oh. God, _ I _ want _ you so bad - ly. And I won - der _____ this: _

Could to-mor-row be _____ so __ won-drous as

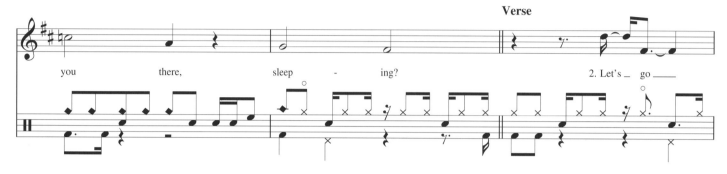

you there, sleep ___ ing? 2. Let's __ go ___

Verse

drive __ till _____ morn-ing __ comes, __ watch __

___ the _____ sun - rise _____ and fill our __ souls _____ up.

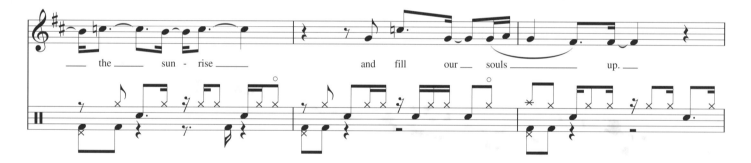

We'll drink __ some _____ wine __ till _____ we __ get __ drunk. __

___ Yeah, _____ it's cra - zy, _____ I'm think-ing, just

Chorus

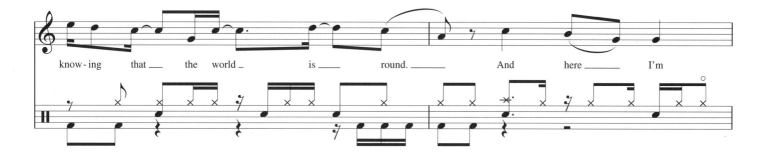

know-ing that ___ the world ___ is ___ round. ___ And ___ here ___ I'm

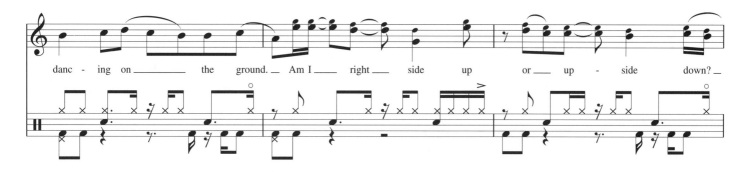

danc-ing on ___ the ground. ___ Am I ___ right ___ side ___ up ___ or ___ up - side ___ down? ___

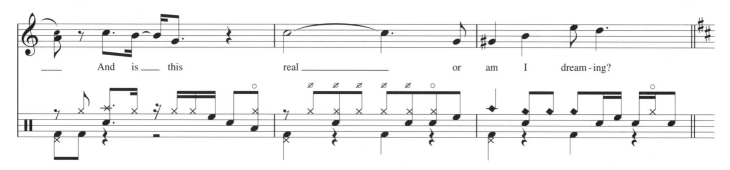

___ And ___ is ___ this ___ real ___ or am I dream-ing?

Pre-Chorus

Love-ly la - dy, ___ let me drink ___ you, ___ please. ___

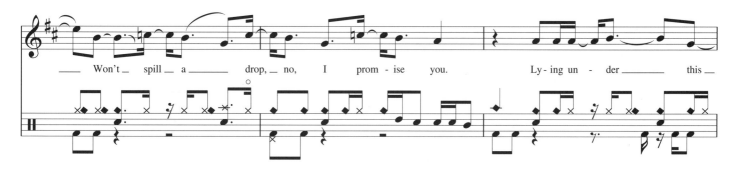

___ Won't ___ spill ___ a ___ drop, ___ no, I prom-ise ___ you. ___ Ly - ing un - der ___ this ___

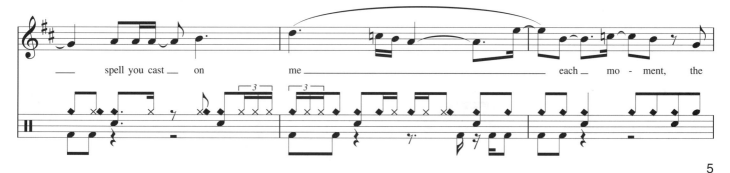

___ spell you cast ___ on ___ me ___ each ___ mo - ment, ___ the

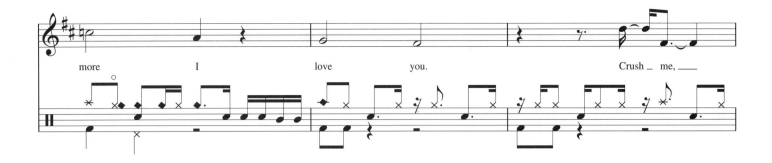

more I love you. Crush me, come on.

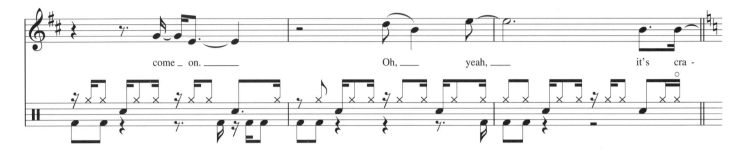

come on. Oh, yeah, it's cra-

Chorus

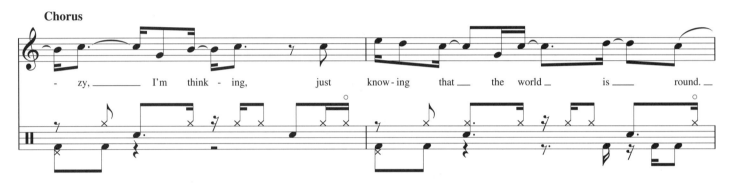

-zy, I'm think-ing, just know-ing that the world is round.

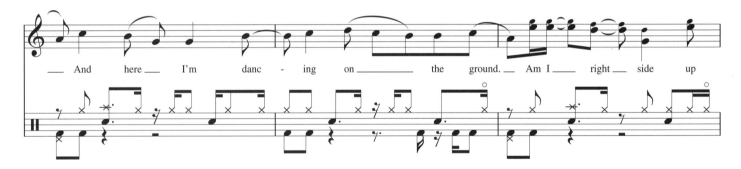

And here I'm danc-ing on the ground. Am I right side up

or up-side down? Is this real, oh, or

Violin Solo

am I dream-ing?

Pre-Chorus

Love- ly la - dy, _____ I will treat __ you sweet - ly, __

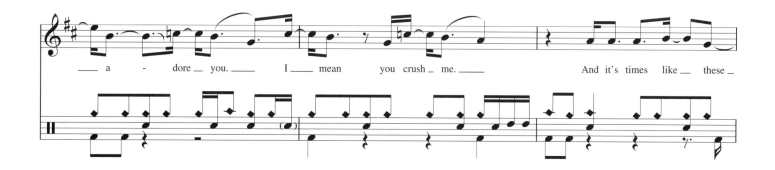

__ a - dore __ you. __ I __ mean you crush __ me. __ And it's times like __ these __

__ when my faith I feel, _____ and __ I __ know

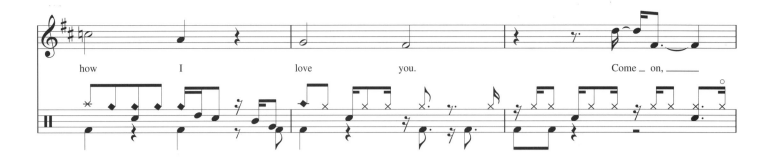

how I love you. Come _ on, _____

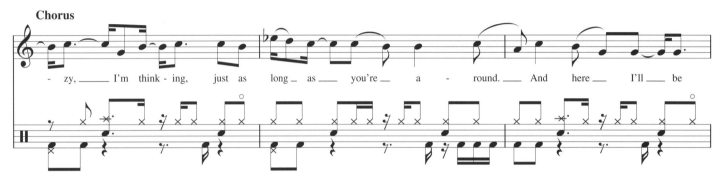

come _ on, _____ ba - by. _____ It's cra -

Chorus

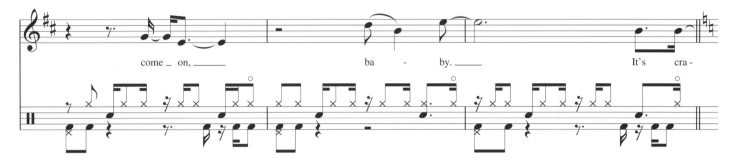

- zy, _____ I'm think - ing, just as long _ as _____ you're _ a - round. _____ And here _ I'll _ be

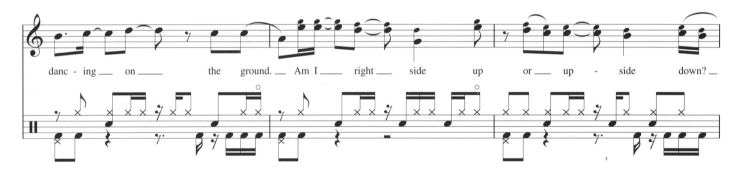

danc - ing _____ on _____ the ground. _ Am I _____ right _____ side up or _____ up - side down? _

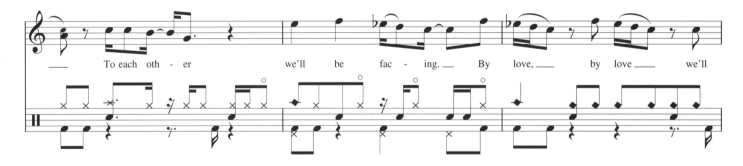

_____ To each oth - er we'll be fac - ing. _____ By love, _____ by love _____ we'll

beat back _ the pain _ we've found. _____ You know, _____ I mean to tell you all _____ the _____ things _

_____ I've been _ think - ing _____ deep in - side. My _ friend, _____ each mo - ment, the

more _ I love you. Crush _ me, _____

come _ on, ba - by. _____

Chorus

So _____ much _____ you _ have

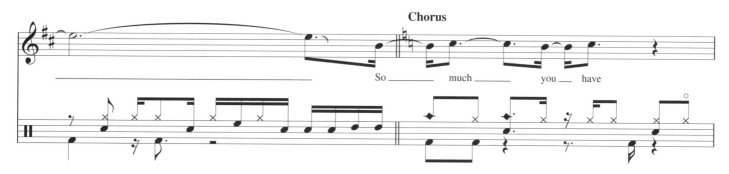

giv - en, love, _____ that I would _ give _____ you back a -

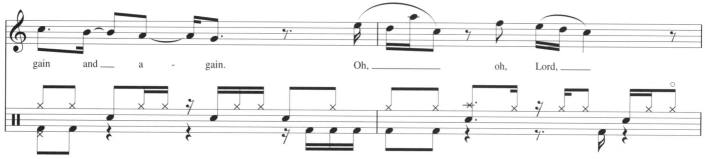

gain and _ a - gain. Oh, _____ oh, Lord, _____

mean - ing I'll ___ hold ___ you. But, please, _____ please, ___ just

let me al - ways...

Outro

Begin fade

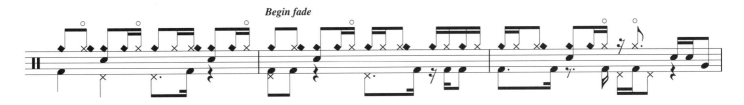

Fade out

DANCING NANCIES

Words and Music by
David J. Matthews

_____ me? Could I have _____ been, _____ oh, _____ an - y-one oth - er than _____

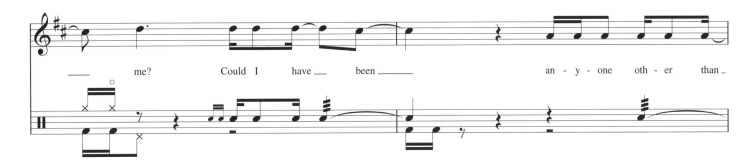

_____ me? Could I have _____ been _____ an - y-one oth - er than _____

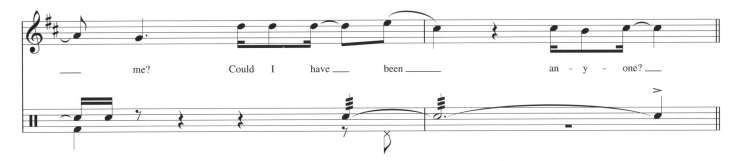

_____ me? Could I have _____ been _____ an - y - one? _____

Faster ♩ = 116

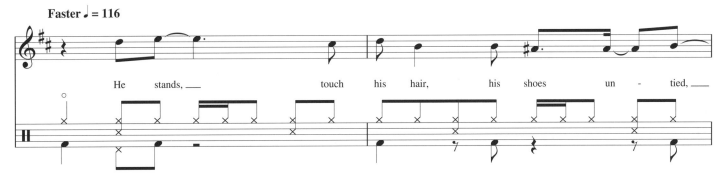

He stands, _____ touch his hair, his shoes un - tied, _____

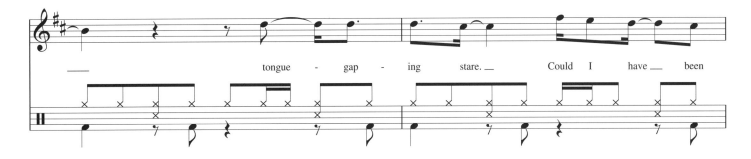

_____ tongue - gap - ing stare. _____ Could I have _____ been

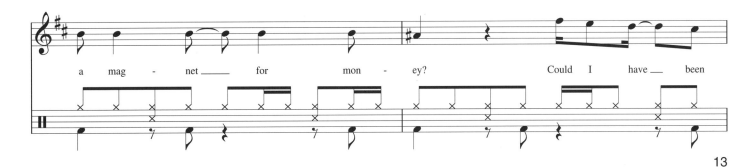

a mag - net _____ for mon - ey? Could I have _____ been

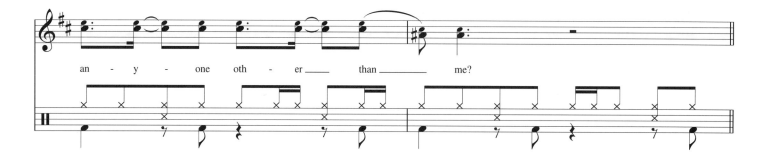

an - y - one oth - er _____ than _____ me?

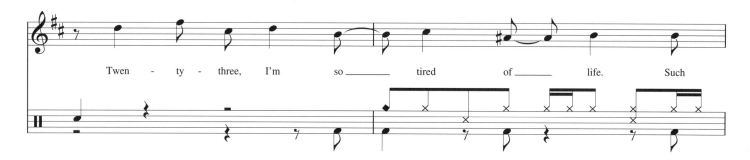

Twen - ty - three, I'm so _____ tired of _____ life. Such

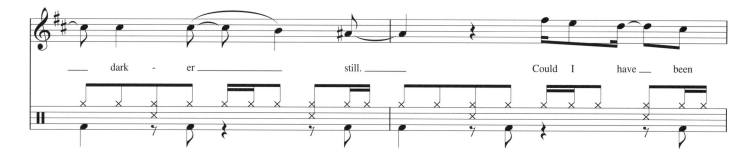

a shame _____ to throw it all _____ a - way. _____ The im - ag - es grow

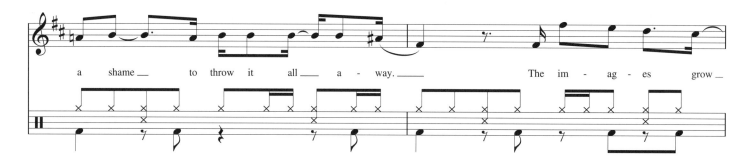

_____ dark - er _____ still. _____ Could I have _____ been

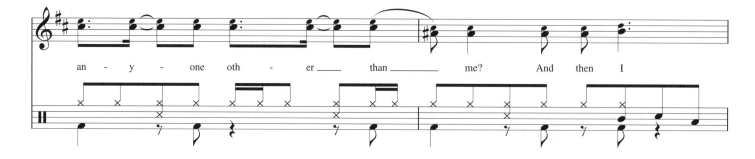

an - y - one oth - er _____ than _____ me? And then I

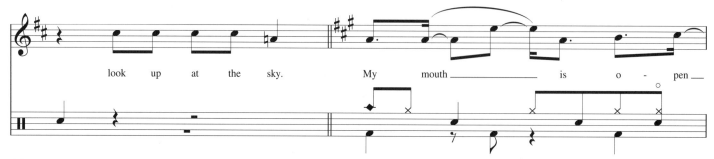

look up at the sky. My mouth _____ is o - pen _____

_____ wide. Lick _____ and taste, what's _____ the use in _____ wor -

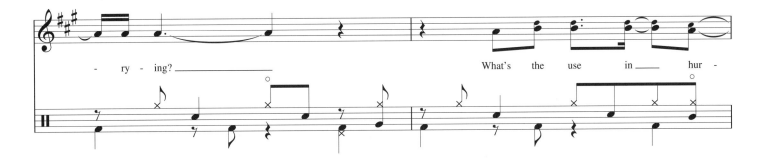

- ry - ing? _____ What's the use in _____ hur -

- ry - ing? _____ Turn, _____ turn, we al - most be - come diz -

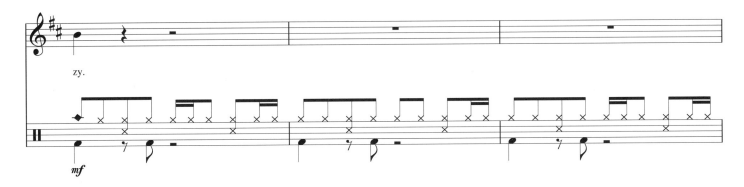

zy.

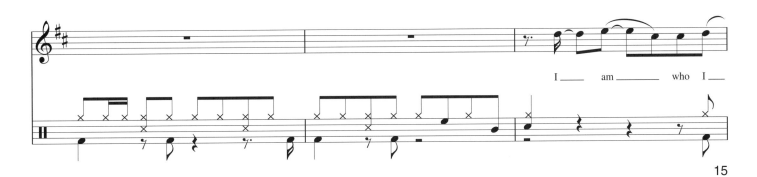

I _____ am _____ who I _____

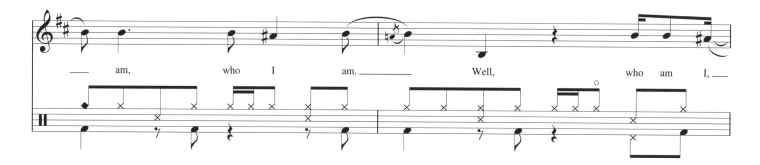

— am, who I am. Well, who am I,

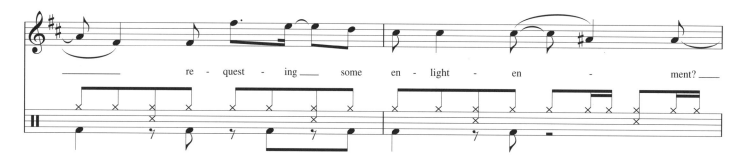

— re - quest - ing some en - light - en - ment? —

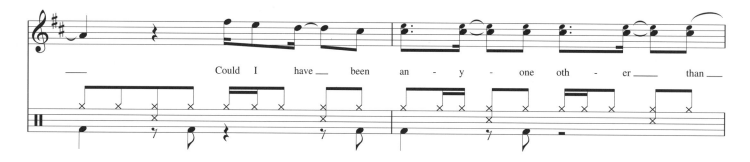

— Could I have been an - y - one oth - er than

— me. And then I'll sing and dance, I'll

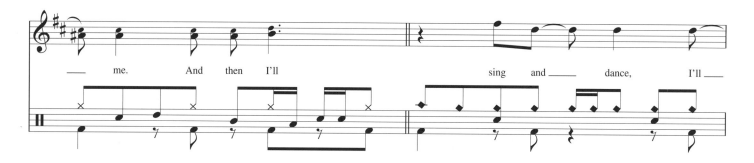

— play for you to - night, the thrill of it

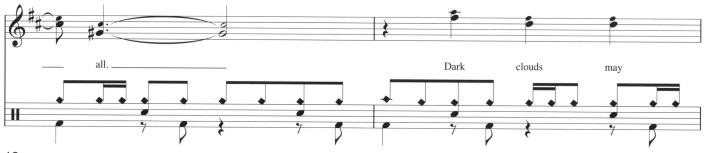

— all. Dark clouds may

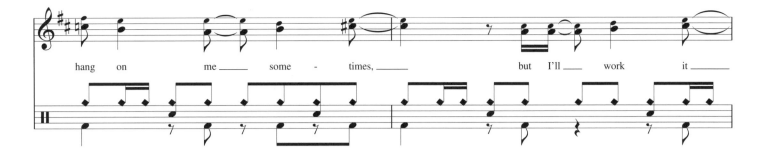

hang on me ___ some - times, ___ but I'll ___ work it ___

___ out. And I look up ___ at the sky. ___

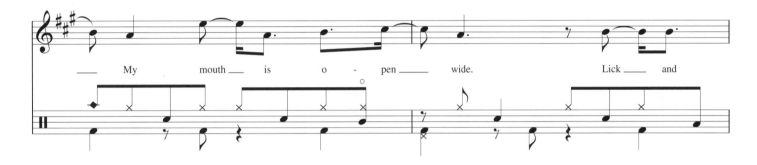

___ My mouth ___ is o - pen ___ wide. Lick ___ and

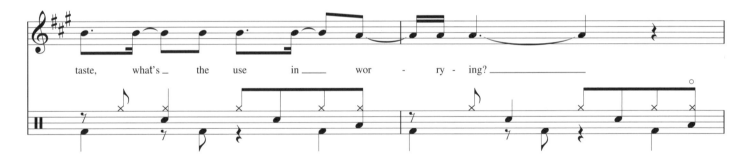

taste, what's ___ the use in ___ wor - ry - ing? _____

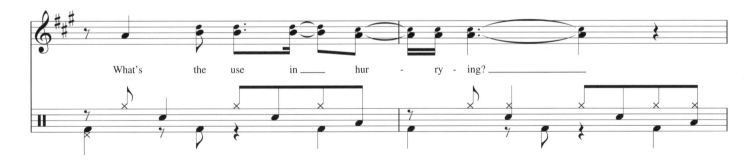

What's ___ the use in ___ hur - ry - ing? _____

Turn, _____ turn, we al - most be - come diz -

zy.

Fall - ing out of _____ a world _____ of _____ lies. _____

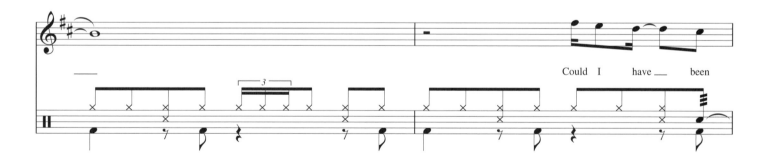

_____ Could I have _____ been

Danc - ing _____ Nan - cy? _____ Ah.

Danc - ing Nan - cy.   Ooh.

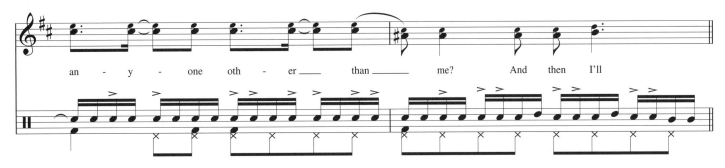

Could I have _ been

an - y - one oth - er _ than _ me? And then I'll

*Bkgd. Voc. Fig. 1

sing and _ dance. _ La   la   la,   hey, _
(La   la   la,   hey, _

*Refers to upstemmed notes only.

End Bkgd. Voc. Fig. 1

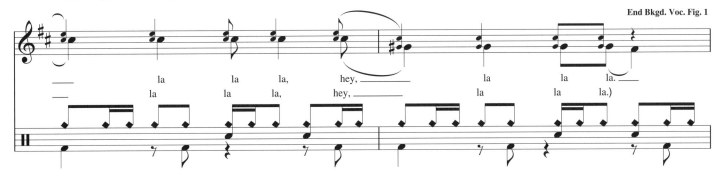

_ la   la   la,   hey, _   la   la   la. _
_ la   la   la,   hey, _   la   la   la.)

w/ Bkgd. Voc. Fig. 1 (3 times)

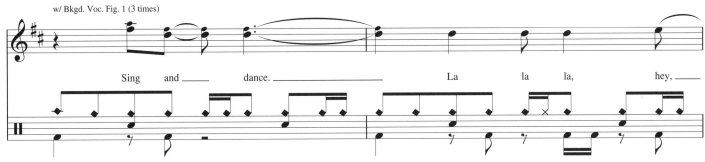

Sing and _ dance. _ La   la   la,   hey, _

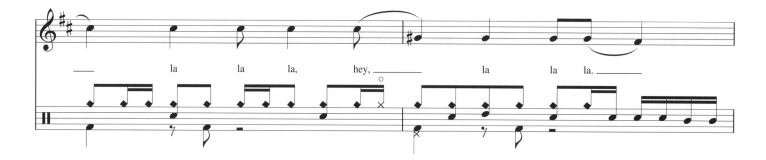

la la la, hey, la la la.

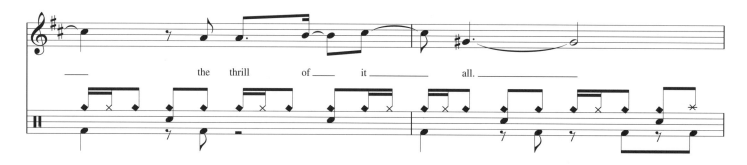

Sing and dance, I'll play for you to - night,

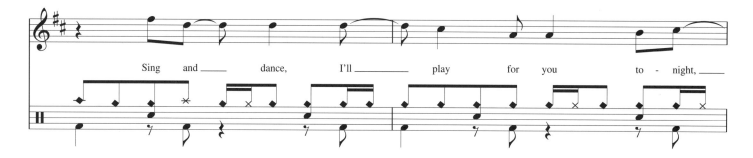

the thrill of it all.

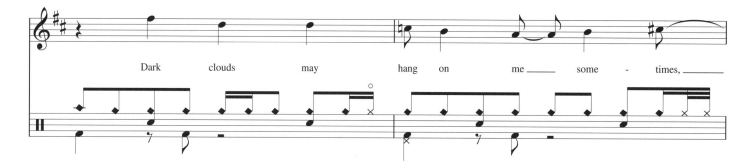

Dark clouds may hang on me some - times,

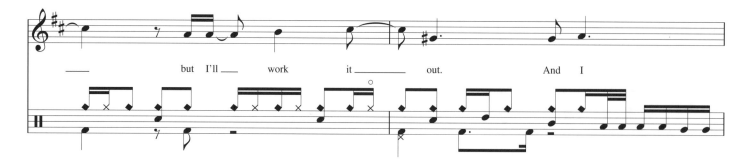

but I'll work it out. And I

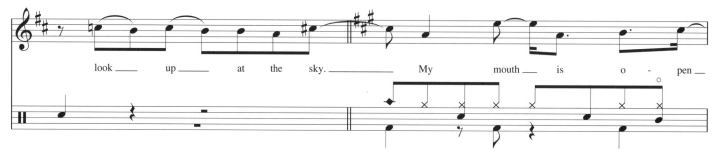

look up at the sky. My mouth is o - pen

_____ wide. Lick _____ and taste, what's _____ the use in _____ wor -

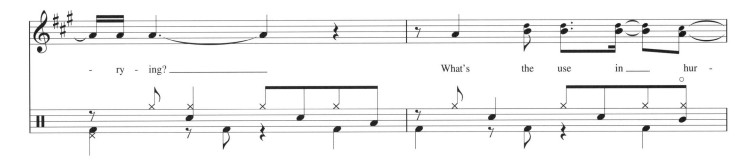

- ry - ing? _____ What's the use in _____ hur -

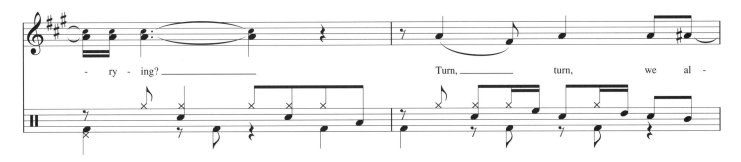

- ry - ing? _____ Turn, _____ turn, we al -

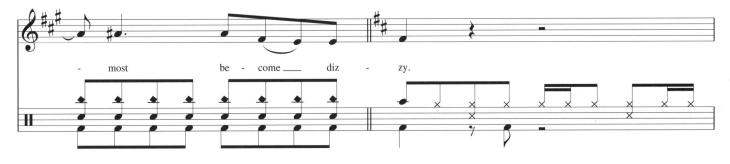

- most be - come _____ diz - zy.

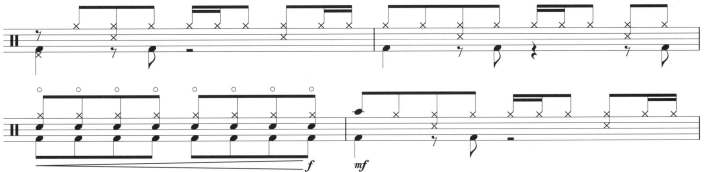

_f_ _mf_

Drums fade out

18

EVERYDAY

Words and Music by
David J. Matthews and Glen Ballard

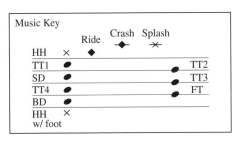

Pick me up, love, ___ hey, ___ oh. ___ Come on, come on, come on, ev-er-y day.

(Pick me up, love, ___ ev-er-y ___ day.)

Snare drum overdub w/ HotRods

mf

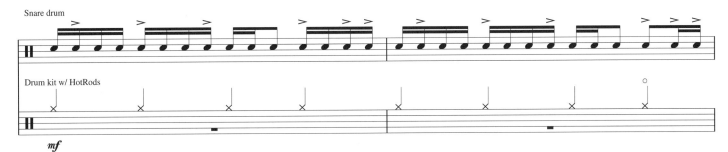

Snare drum

Drum kit w/ HotRods

mf

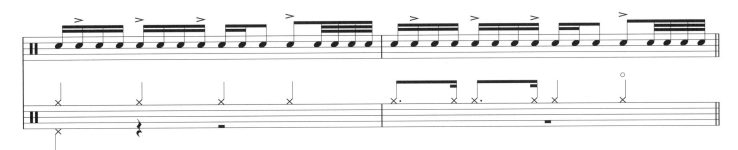

Verse

1. Pick me up, love, ___ from the ___ bot-tom

up _____ to the top, love, ev - er - y ____ day. _____

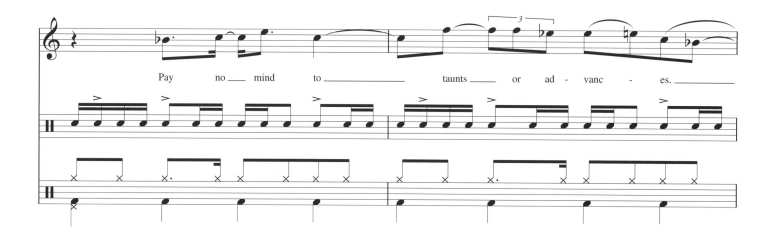

Pay no ___ mind to _____ taunts ____ or ad - vanc - es. _____

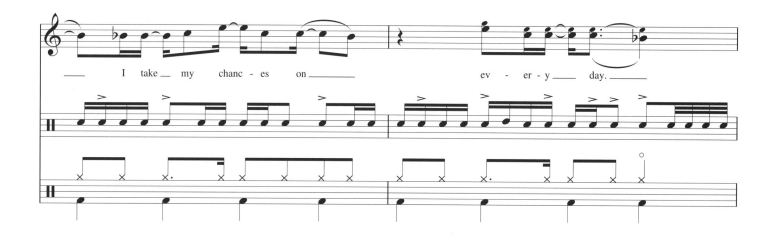

____ I take ___ my chanc - es on _____ ev - er - y ____ day. _____

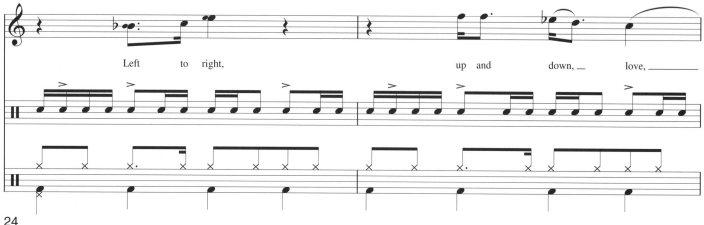

Left to right, up and down, ___ love, _____

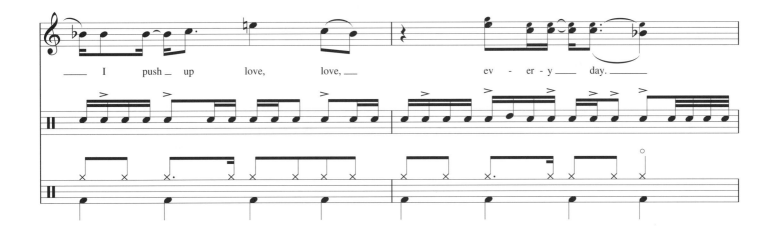

I push up love, love, ev - er - y day.

Jump in the mud, oh, get your hands dirt - y with...

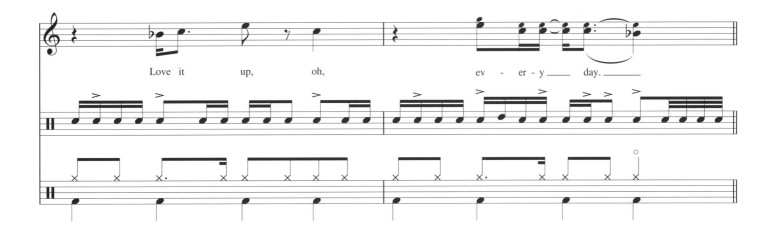

Love it up, oh, ev - er - y day.

Chorus

Snare drum tacet

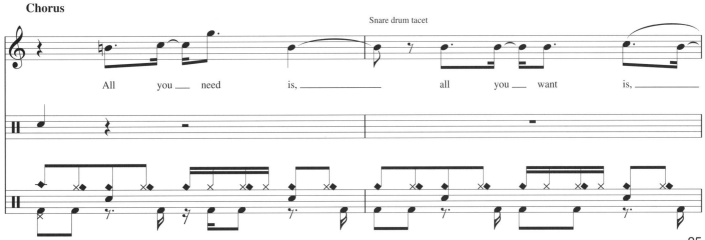

All you need is, all you want is,

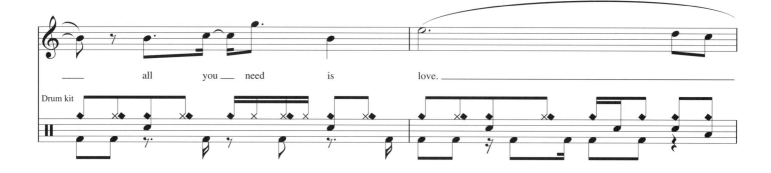

all you _____ need _____ is _____ love. _____

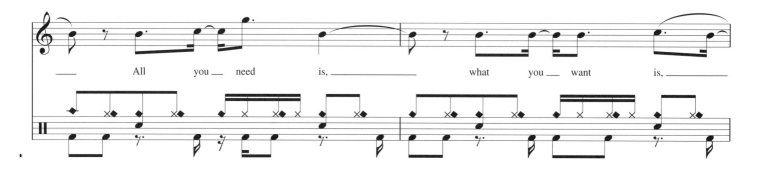

All _____ you _____ need _____ is, _____ what _____ you _____ want _____ is, _____

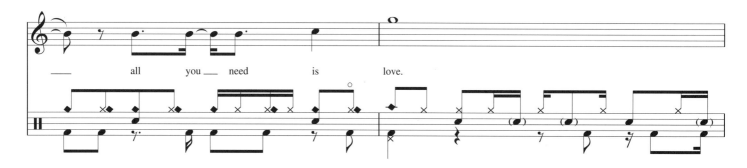

all _____ you _____ need _____ is _____ love.

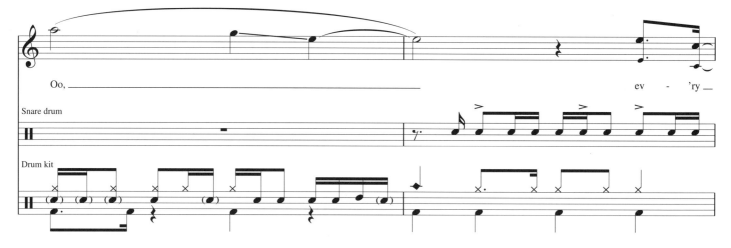

Oo, _____ ev - 'ry _____

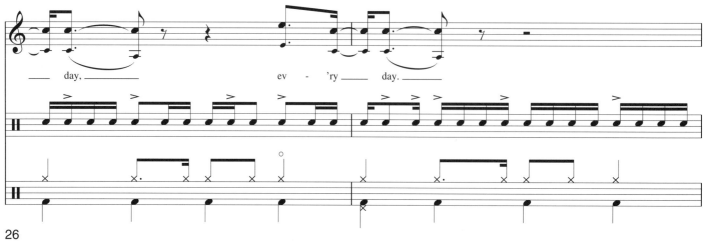

_____ day, _____ ev - 'ry _____ day.

Verse

Oh, _____ ev - 'ry __ day. 2. Pick me up, love, _____

_____ from the bot - tom ___ up on _____ to the top, love, ___

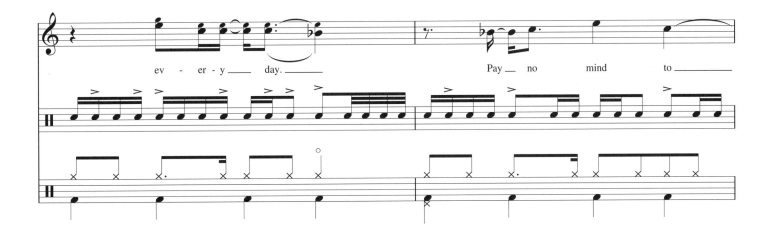

ev - er - y __ day. _____ Pay _ no mind to _____

_____ taunts _____ or ad - vanc - es. I'm _ gon - na take my _ chanc - es on

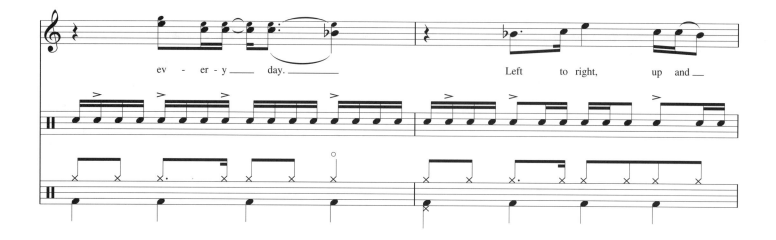

ev - er - y _____ day. _____ Left to right, up and _____

up and in - side _____ out _____ right, _____ good love _____ fight _____ for _____

ev - er - y _____ day. _____ Jump in the mud, _____ mud, _____

get your _____ hands filth - y, love. _____ Give it up, love, _____

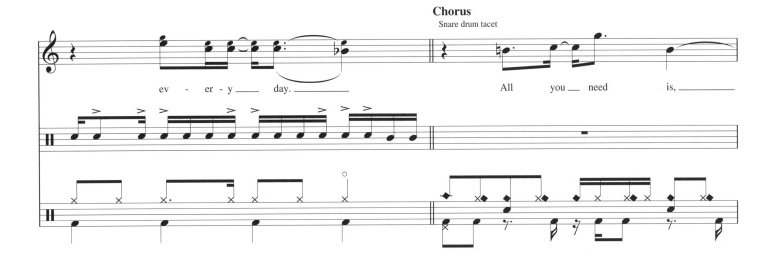

ev - er - y___ day. _____ All you ___ need is, _____

___ all you ___ want is, _____ all you ___ need is

Drum kit

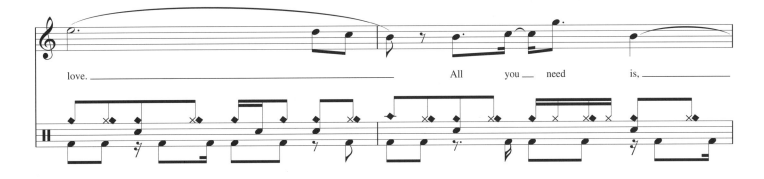

love. _____ All you ___ need is, _____

___ what you ___ want is, _____ all you ___ need is

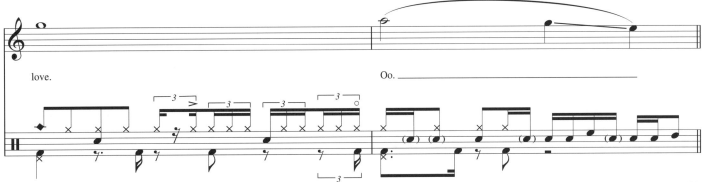

love. _____ Oo. _____

Bridge

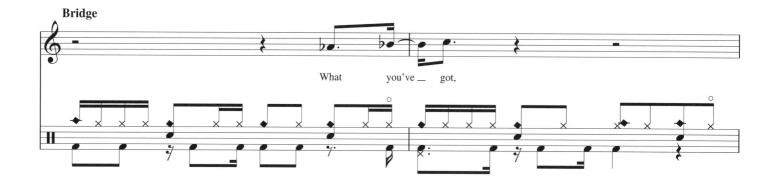

What you've ___ got,

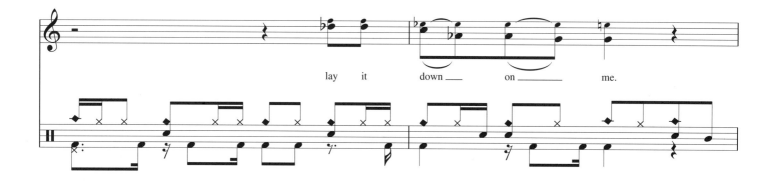

lay it down ___ on ___ me.

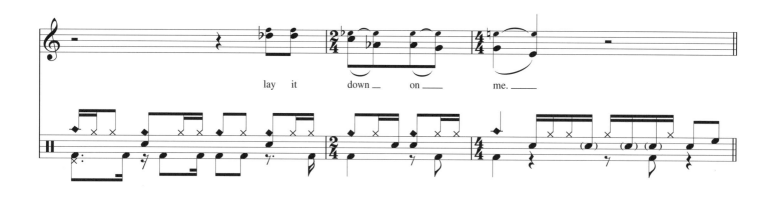

What you've ___ got,

lay it down ___ on ___ me. ___

Chorus

All you ___ need is, ___ all you ___ want is, ___

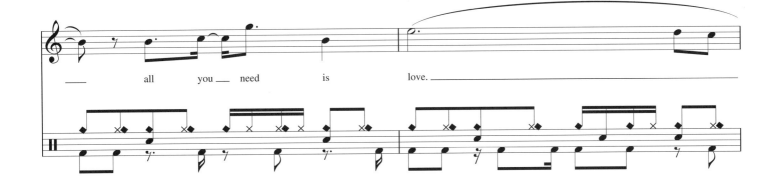

all you need is love.

All you need is, what you want is,

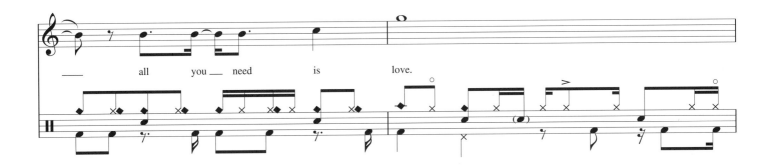

all you need is love.

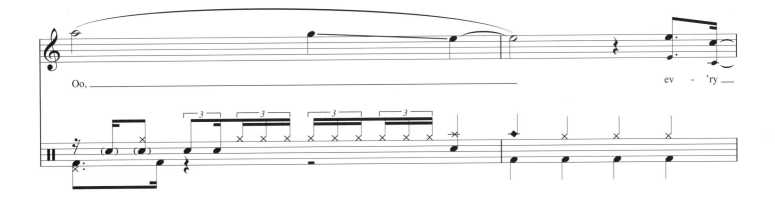

Oo, ev - 'ry

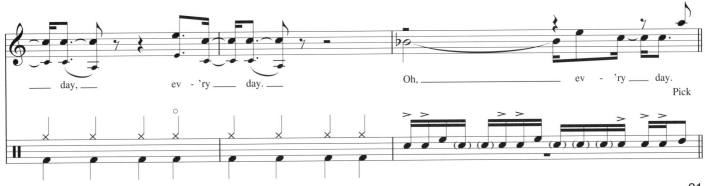

day, ev - 'ry day. Oh, ev - 'ry day. Pick

Outro

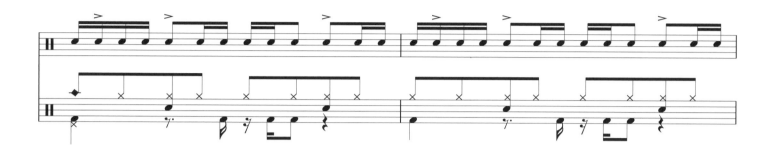

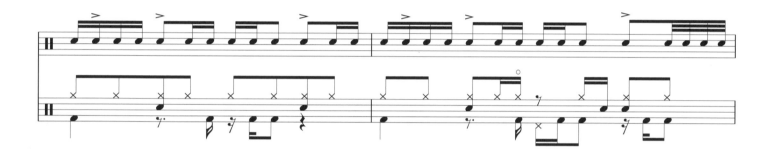

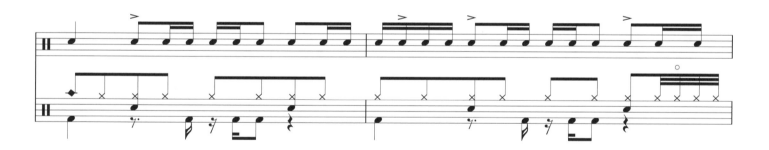

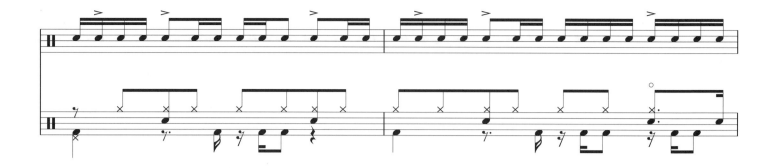

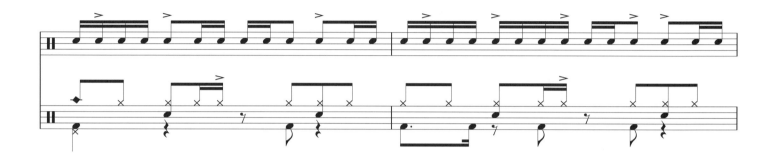

GREY STREET

Lyrics by David J. Matthews
Music by Dave Matthews Band

Intro

Moderately slow ♩ = 108

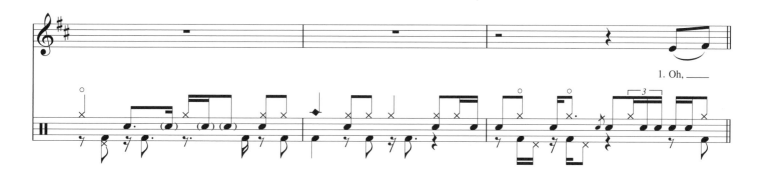

1. Oh, ___

Verse

look at how ___ she lis - tens, she ___ says noth-

- ing of what she thinks. She just ___ goes

stum - bling _____ through her mem - o - ries, star - ing out _____

_____ on - to Grey _____ Street. _____ And she _____ thinks, "Hey. _____

_____ How did _____ I come _____

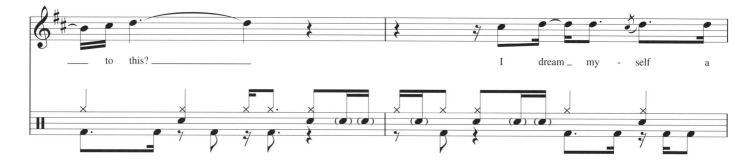

_____ to this? _____ I dream _ my - self a

thou - sand _ times _ a - round _ the world, _____ but I can't get

out of this _____ place." _____ Mm, there's an

Chorus

emp - ti - ness _____ in - side _____ her and she'd do

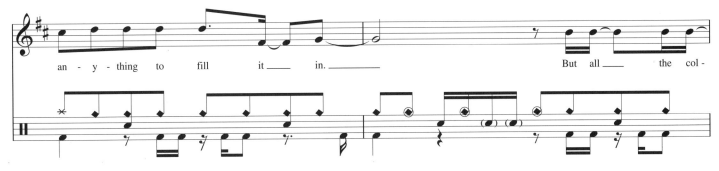

an - y - thing to fill it _____ in. _____ But all _____ the col -

- ors _____ mix to - geth - er to grey. _____

And it breaks _____

_____ her heart. _____ 2. How she

Verse

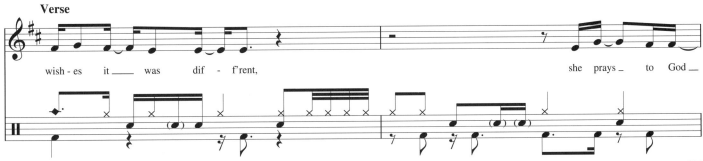

wish - es it _____ was dif - f'rent, she prays _ to God _

most ___ ev - 'ry night. And though ___ she

swears it does - n't lis - ten, there's still a hope ___

___ in her it might. She says, "I pray, ___

oh, ___ but they ___ fall ___

___ on deaf ears. ___ Am I sup - posed to

take it on ___ my - self ___ to get ___ out of

this place?" _____ Oh, there's a

Chorus

lone - li - ness _____ in - side _____ her and she'd do

an - y - thing to fill it _____ in. _____ And though it's

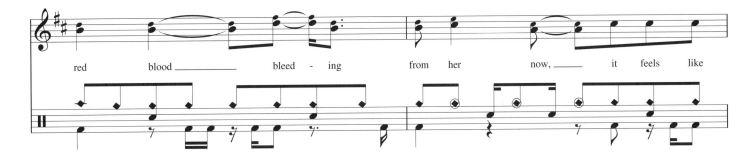

red blood _____ bleed - ing from her now, _____ it feels like

cold blue ice _____ in her _____ heart _____ when all _____ the col -

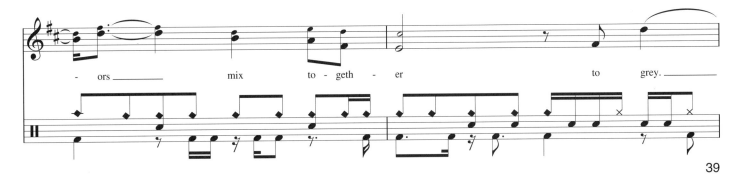

- ors _____ mix to - geth - er to grey. _____

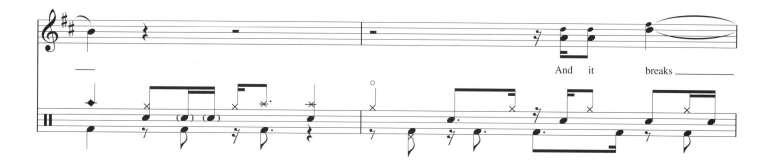

And it breaks _____

_____ her heart. _____ 3. There's a

Verse

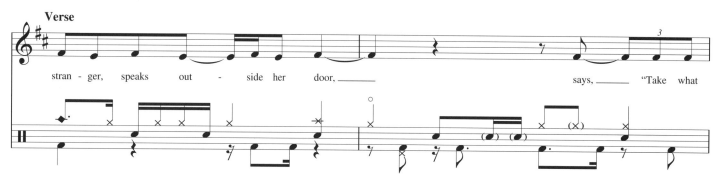

stran - ger, speaks out - side her door, _____ says, _____ "Take what

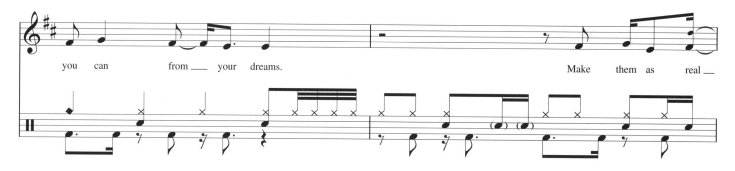

you can from ___ your dreams. Make them as real ___

___ as an - y - thing. ___ Oh, it - 'd take ___ the work ___

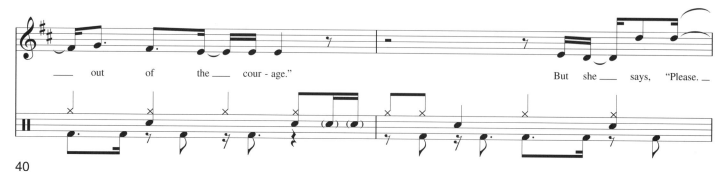

___ out of the ___ cour - age." But she ___ says, "Please. ___

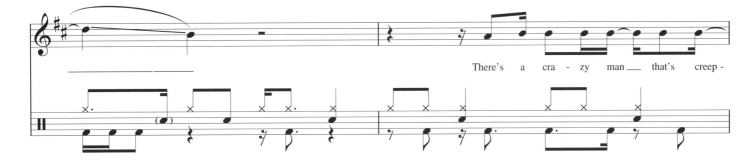

There's a cra - zy man ___ that's creep -

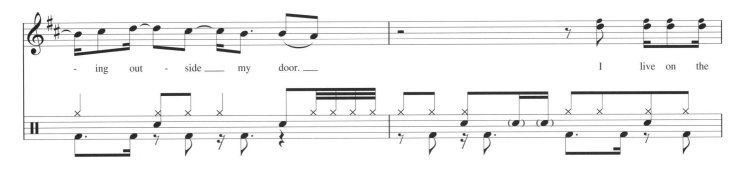

- ing out - side ___ my door. ___

I live on the

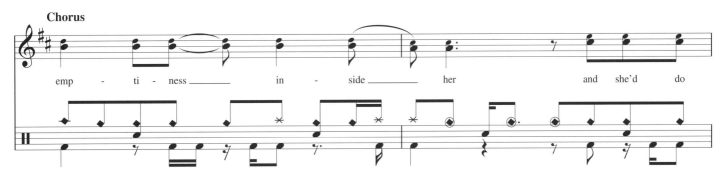

cor - ner of ___ Grey ___ Street ___

and the end ___

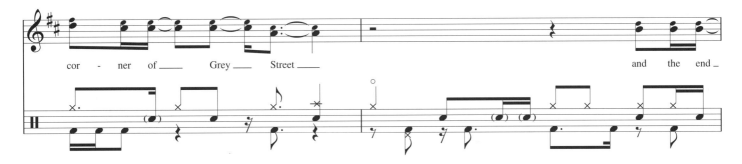

___ of the world." ___

Oh, there's an

Chorus

emp - ti - ness ___ in - side ___ her

and she'd do

an - y - thing to fill it ___ in. ___

And though it's

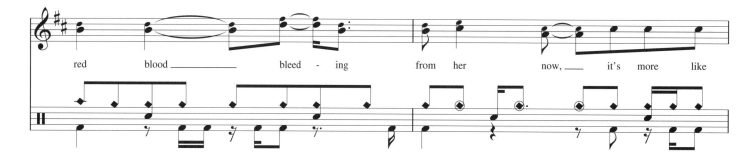

red blood _____ bleed - ing from her now, ____ it's more like

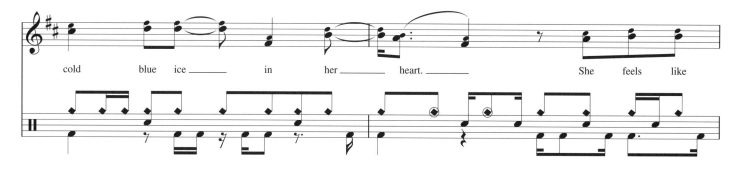

cold blue ice _____ in her _____ heart. _____ She feels like

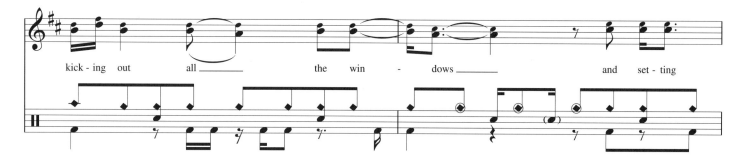

kick - ing out all _____ the win - dows _____ and set - ting

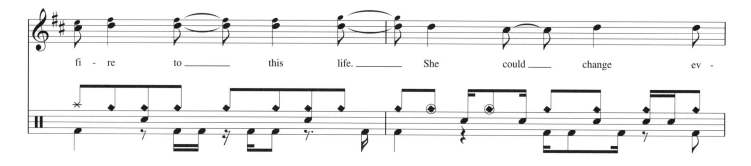

fi - re to _____ this life. _____ She could ____ change ev -

'ry - thing a - bout _____ her _____ us - ing

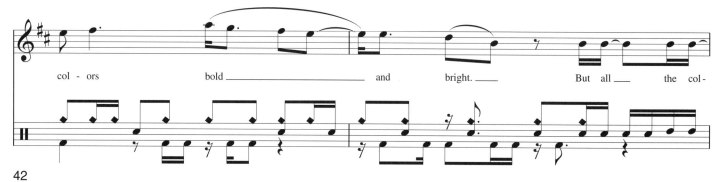

col - ors bold _____ and bright. ____ But all ___ the col -

-ors _____ mix to-geth - er to grey. _____

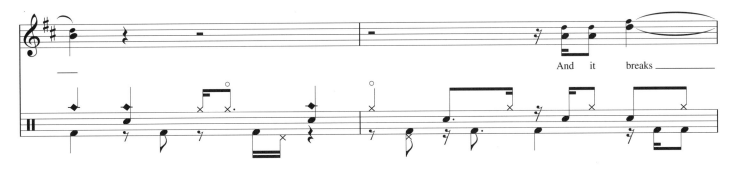

And it breaks _____

_____ her heart. _____ Oh, it breaks _____

_____ her heart _____ to grey. _____

Outro

Yeah. _____

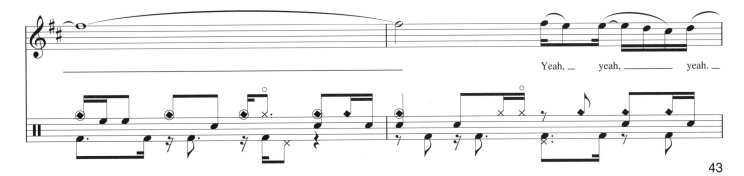

Yeah, ___ yeah, _____ yeah. _____

No.

Begin fade

Fade out

JIMI THING

Words and Music by
David J. Matthews

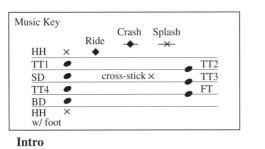

Intro

Moderately ♩ = 100

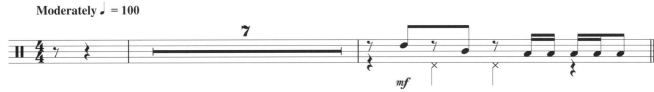

Verse

1. Late - ly I've been feel - in' low, a rem - e - dy

is what I'm seek - in'. I

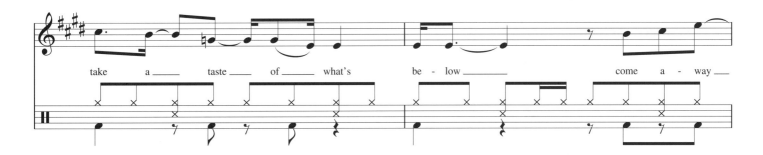

take a taste of what's be - low come a - way

to some - thing bet - ter.

What _ I _ want _ is what I've not _ got, but what I

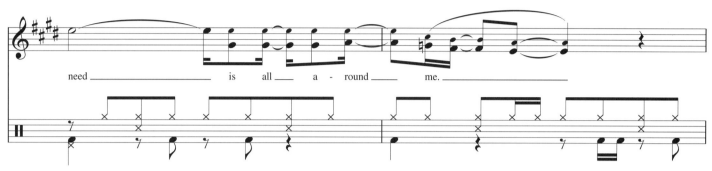

need _ is all _ a - round _ me. _

Reach - ing, search - ing, _ nev - er stop and I'll

Pre-Chorus

say... _ If you _ could keep _ me float -

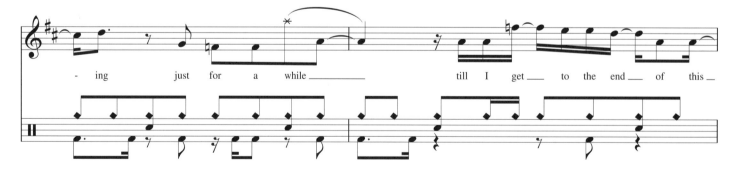

- ing just for a while _ till I get _ to the end _ of this _

_ tun - nel, oh, Mom - my. _ If you _ could keep _ me float -

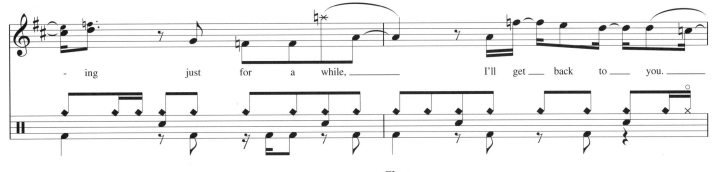

-ing just for a while, _____ I'll get back to _____ you. _____

Chorus

_____ Some - time a Jim - i _____ thing

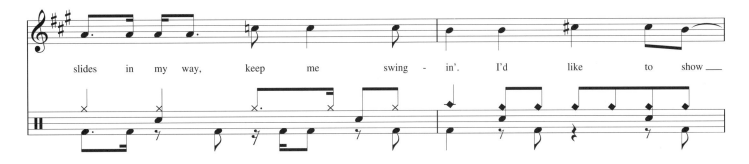

slides in my way, keep me swing - in'. I'd like to show _____

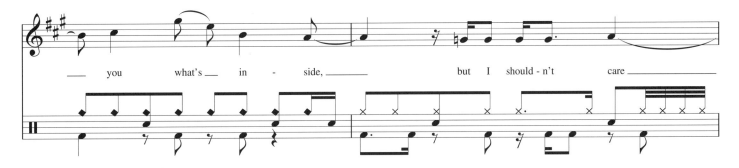

_____ you what's _____ in - side, _____ but I should - n't care _____

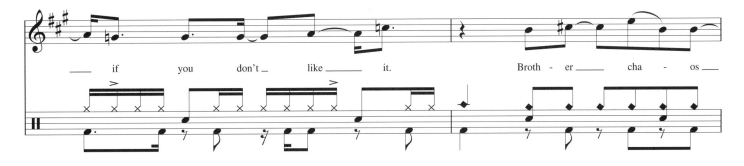

_____ if you don't _____ like _____ it. Broth - er _____ cha - os _____

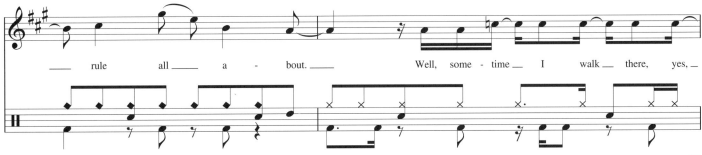

_____ rule all _____ a - bout. _____ Well, some - time _____ I walk there, yes, _____

God knows_ some - time I take a bus_ there._ Should - n't_ care, I

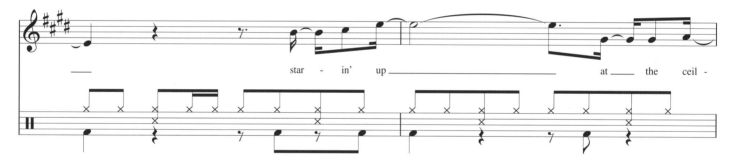

should - n't care,_ be - reaved_ as I'm feel - in'._

Verse

2. The day_ is gone,_ I'm on_ my back,_

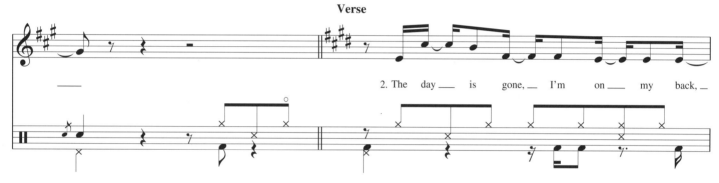

star - in' up_____ at_ the ceil -

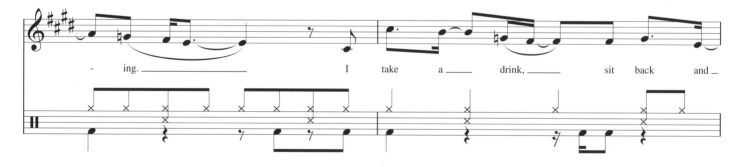

- ing._____ I take a_ drink,_ sit back and_

__ re - lax,_ smoke_ my mind_____ to make me feel

bet - ter for a small time. What I want is what I've

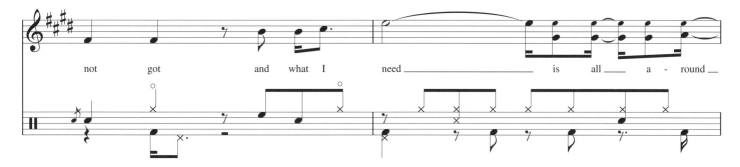

not got and what I need is all a - round

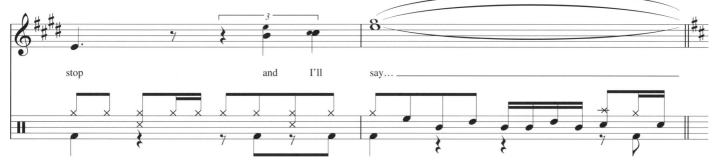

me. Reach - ing, search - ing, nev - er

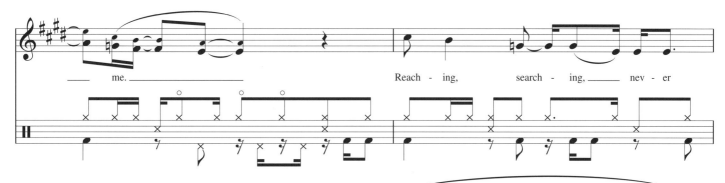

stop and I'll say...

Pre-Chorus

If you could keep me float - ing just for a while

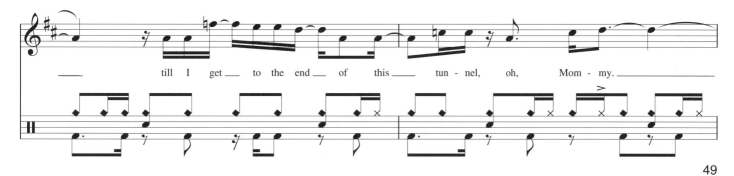

till I get to the end of this tun - nel, oh, Mom - my.

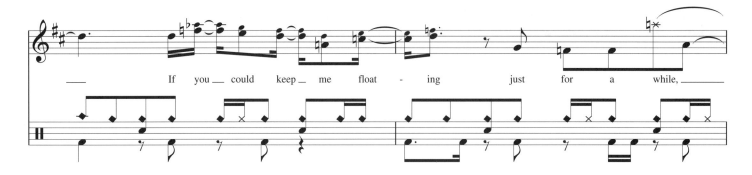

If you __ could keep __ me float - ing just for a while, __

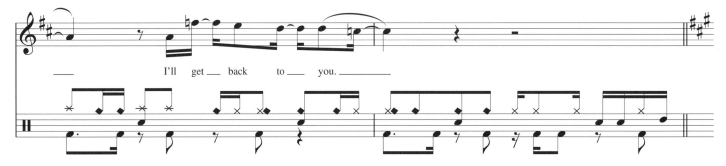

I'll get __ back to __ you. __

Chorus

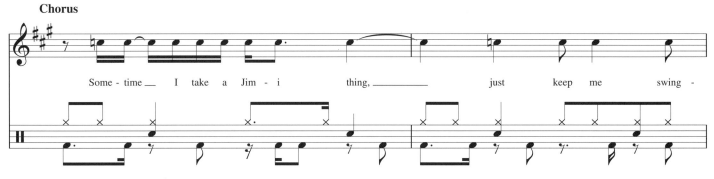

Some - time __ I take a Jim - i thing, __ just keep me swing -

in'. I'd like to show __ you what's __ in - side, __

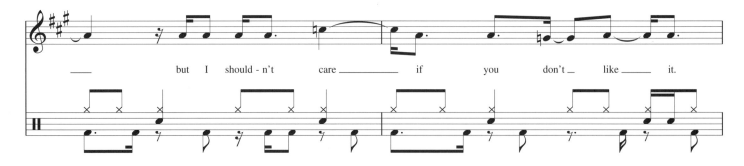

__ but I should - n't care __ if you don't __ like __ it.

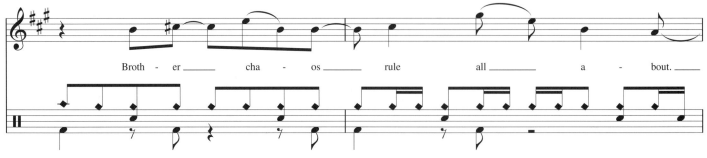

Broth - er __ cha - os __ rule all __ a - bout. __

Well, some - time ___ I walk ___ there, yes, ___ God ___ knows ___ some - time I take a bus ___ there. ___

Should - n't ___ care, I should - n't care, ___ be - reaved ___

___ as I'm feel - in'. ___

Violin solo

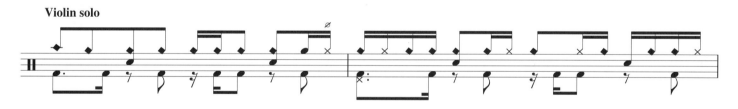

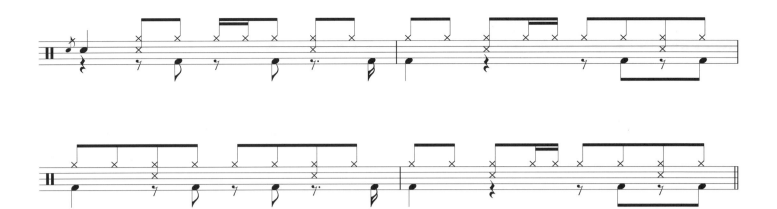

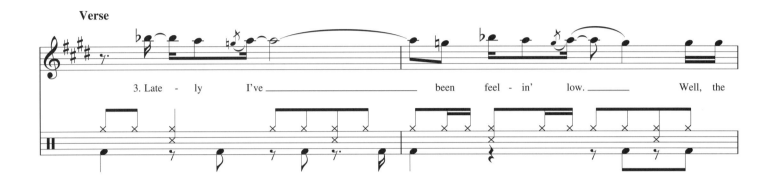

Verse

3. Late - ly I've _____ been feel - in' low. _____ Well, the

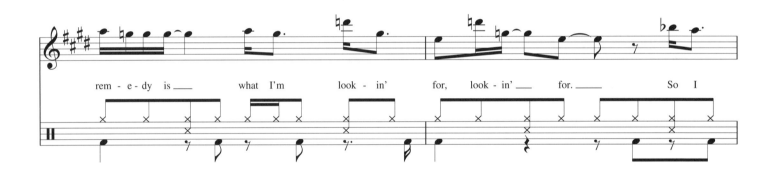

rem - e - dy is ____ what I'm look - in' for, look - in' ___ for. _____ So I

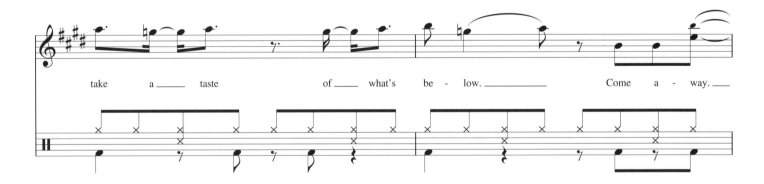

take a ____ taste of ____ what's be - low. _____ Come a - way. ___

Pre-Chorus

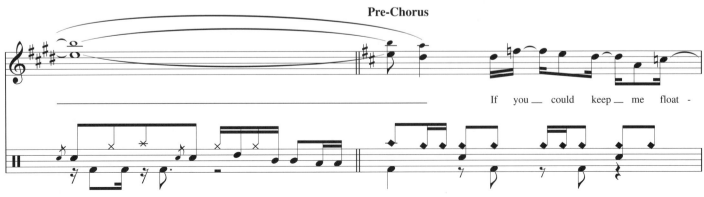

If you __ could keep __ me float -

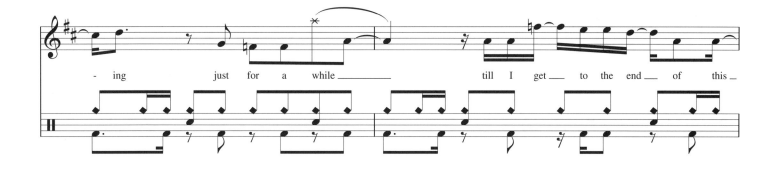

-ing   just for a while _____   till I get _____ to the end ____ of this _____

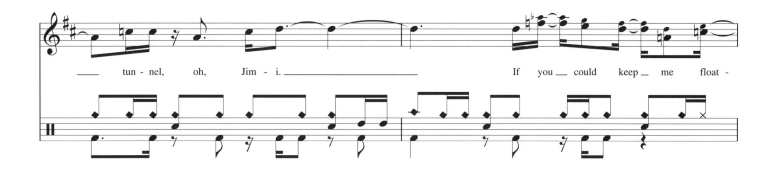

_____ tun - nel,   oh,   Jim - i. _____   If you ____ could keep ___ me float -

-ing   just for a   while, _____   I'll get ____ back   to ____ you. _____

Chorus

_____ Some-time ____ I take a Jim - i   thing, _____

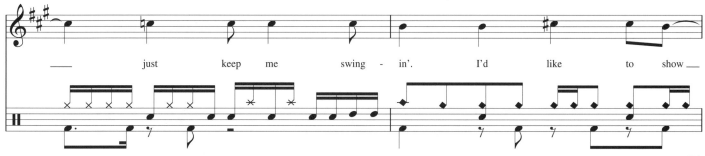

_____ just   keep   me   swing - in'.   I'd   like   to   show ____

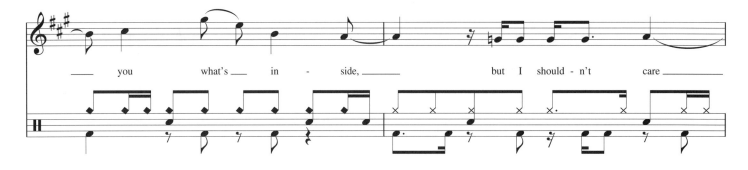

you what's in -side, _____ but I should -n't care _____

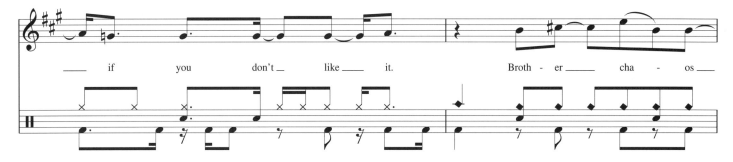

if you don't like it. Broth- er cha -os

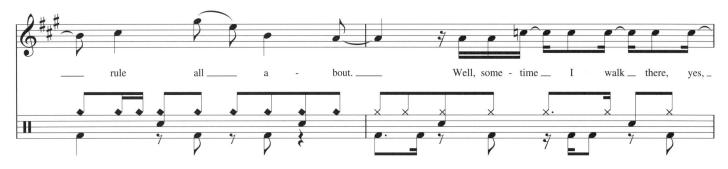

rule all a - bout. _____ Well, some- time I walk there, yes, _

God knows some- time I take a bus there. _____ Should -n't care, I

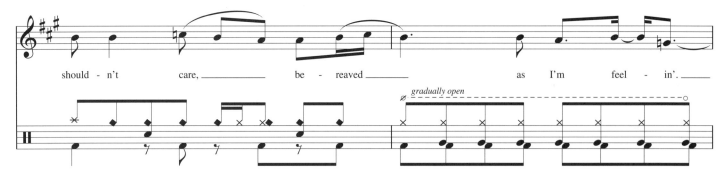

should -n't care, _____ be - reaved _____ as I'm feel- in'. _____

gradually open

Sax Solo

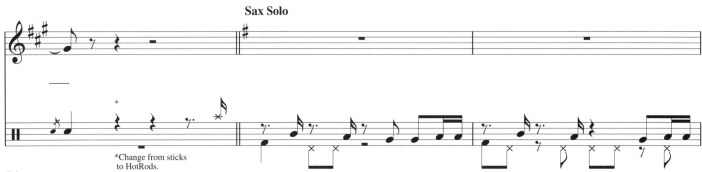

*Change from sticks
  to HotRods.

54

Begin fade

Fade out

THE SPACE BETWEEN

Words and Music by
David J. Matthews and Glen Ballard

*Drums tacet till Chorus.

**Sequenced sample (Ride plus noise) played throughout Choruses.

we tell and hope ___ to keep ___ us safe from the pain. ___

Verse

But will I hold you a - gain? 2. These fick - le, fud - dled words ___ con -

- fuse ___ me, ___ like "Will it rain ___ to - day?"

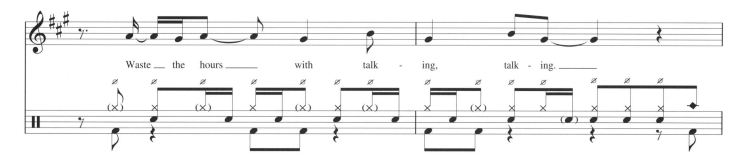

Waste ___ the hours ___ with talk - ing, talk - ing. ___

Chorus

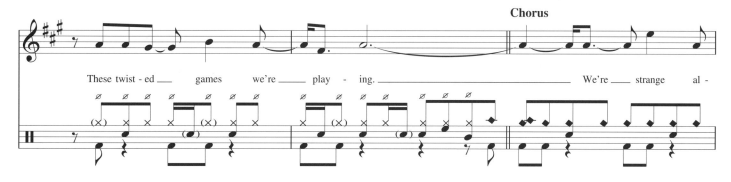

These twist - ed ___ games we're play - ing. ___ We're ___ strange al -

lies with war - ring hearts. ___ What a wild ___ eyed ___ beast you ___ be. ___

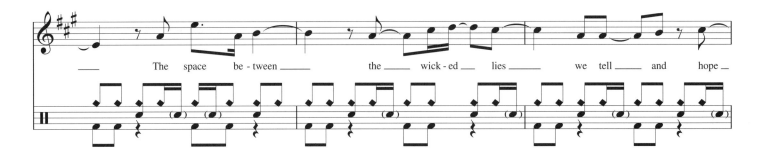

The space be-tween ____ the ____ wick-ed ____ lies ____ we tell ____ and hope ____

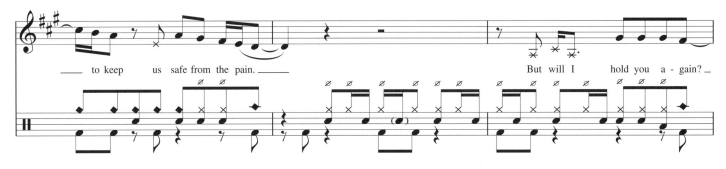

____ to keep us safe from the pain. ____ But will I hold you a-gain? ____

Bridge

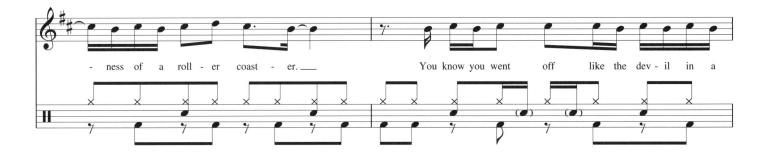

____ Will I hold... ____ Look at us spin-ning out in the mad-

-ness of a roll-er coast-er. ____ You know you went off like the dev-il in a

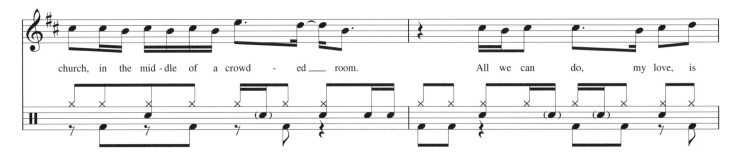

church, in the mid-dle of a crowd-ed ____ room. All we can do, my love, is

Chorus

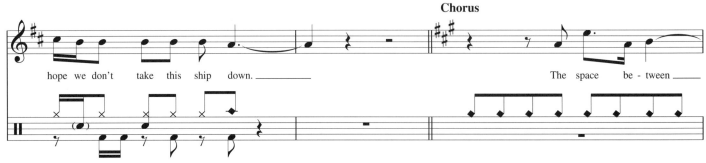

hope we don't take this ship down. ____ The space be-tween ____

where you __ smile __ and hide ____ is where you'll find __ me if I __ get to go. __

__ The space be-tween ____ the bul-lets in our fi - re fight ____ is where

I'll be hid-ing, wait-ing for you. ____ The rain that falls ____ splashed __ in your heart, __

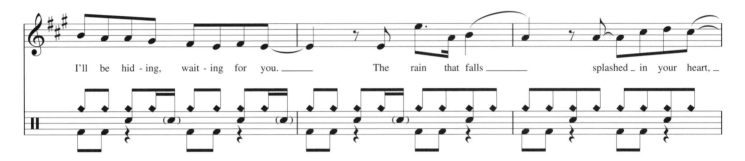

____ ran ____ like sad - ness __ down the win - dow in - to your

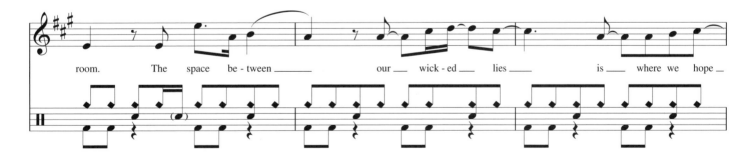

room. The space be - tween ____ our __ wick - ed __ lies ____ is __ where we hope __

__ to keep safe __ from pain. ____ Take my __ hand __ 'cause __ we're walk - ing ____

out _____ of _____ here. _____ Oh,

oh. ____ Right out __ of here, _____ love __ is all _____ we need, __ dear. ____

Outro-Chorus

The space be - tween _____ what's _ wrong and right _____ is where _ you'll find _

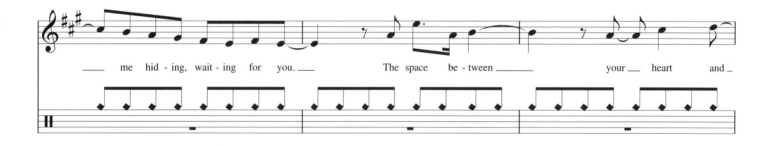

____ me hid - ing, wait - ing for you. __ The space be - tween _____ your __ heart and _

____ mind _____ is the space ___ we'll fill with time. ____ The space be - tween. ____

Repeat and fade

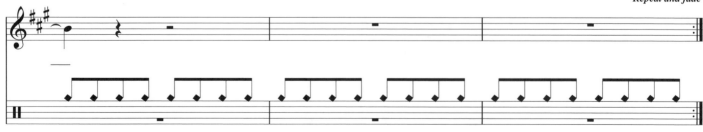

TRIPPING BILLIES

Words and Music by
David J. Matthews

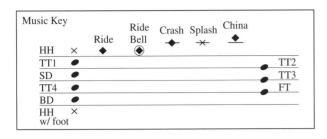

Moderately ♩ = 124

Verse

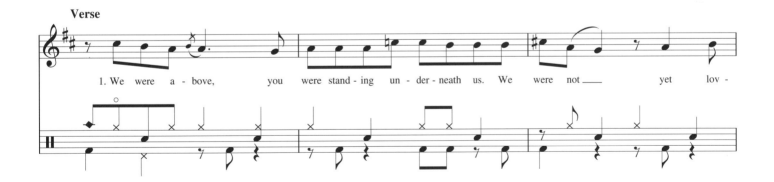

1. We were a- bove, you were stand-ing un- der- neath us. We were not ___ yet lov-

ers.

Drag- ons were smoked, bum- ble- bees were sting- ing us. I was ___

soon ___ to be cra - zy. Eat, drink ___ and be mer - ry, ___

___ for ___ to - mor - row ___ we ___ die. ___ Eat, drink ___

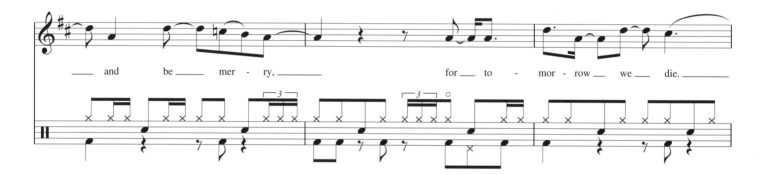

___ and be ___ mer - ry, ___ for ___ to - mor - row ___ we ___ die. ___

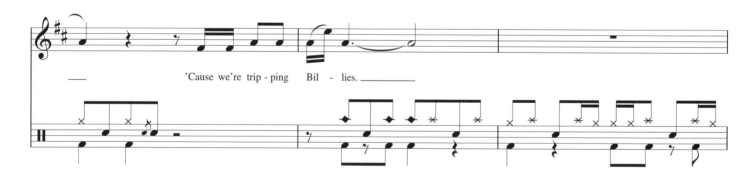

'Cause we're trip - ping Bil - lies. ___

Verse

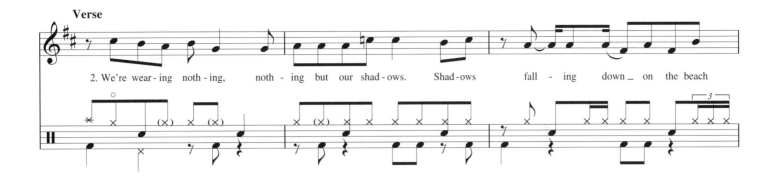

2. We're wear-ing noth-ing, noth-ing but our shad-ows. Shad-ows fall-ing down on the beach

sand. Re-mem-b'ring once, out on the beach-es. We wore

Chorus

pine-ap-ple grass brace-lets. So why would you care

to get out of this place? You and me

and all our friends, such a hap-py hu-man race,

yeah.

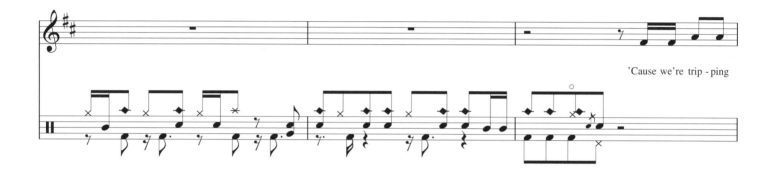

'Cause we're trip - ping

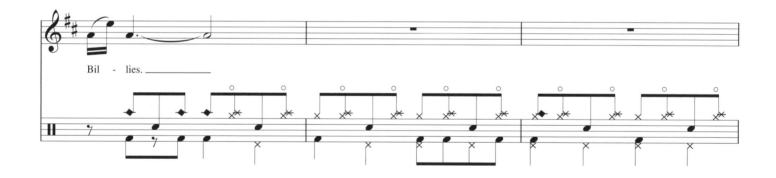

Bil - lies. _____

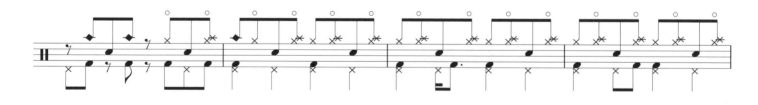

Verse

3. We are all sit - ting, ___ legs ___ crossed 'round ___ a fire. ___

Chorus

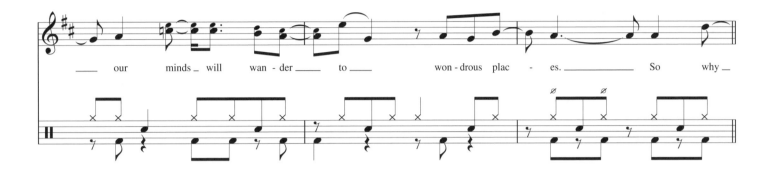

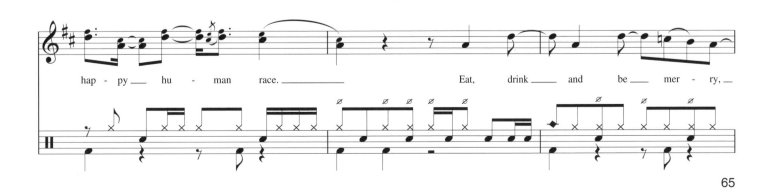

for — to - mor - row — we — die. _____ Eat, drink —

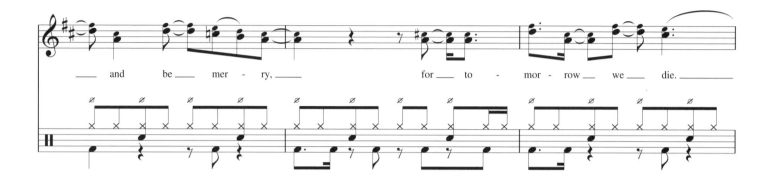

— and — be — mer - ry, _____ for — to - mor - row — we — die. _____

Violin Solo

— Take it, moun - tain boy, _____ yeah.

Oh, _____ eat, drink ____

Chorus

____ and be ____ mer - ry, ____ for ____ to - mor - row ____ we die. ____

Eat, drink ____ and be ____ mer - ry, ____ for ____ to -

mor - row ____ we ____ die. ____ Eat, drink ____

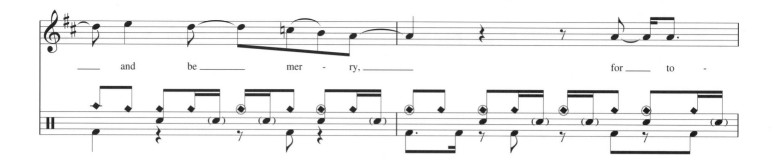

_____ and be _____ mer - ry, _____ for _____ to -

mor - row _____ we _____ die. _____ Eat, drink _____

_____ and be _____ mer - ry, _____ for _____ to -

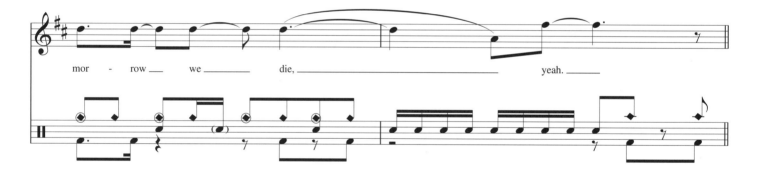

mor - row _____ we _____ die, _____ yeah. _____

Outro

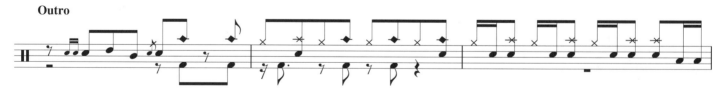

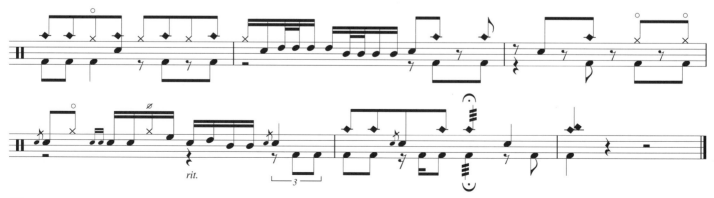

rit.

3

TWO STEP

Words and Music by
David J. Matthews

what   I'm _____ seek - ing. _____ Say,   love,   you

drive ____ me   to   dis - trac - tion. ___

Verse

2. Oh, _____ hey,   my ___

w/ Drum Fig. 1 (8 times)

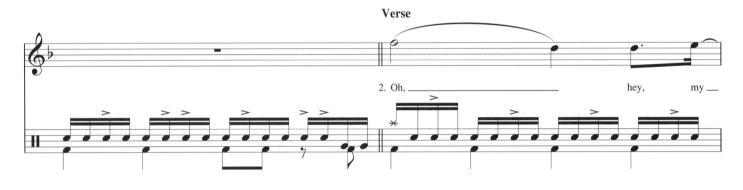

____ love,   do   you ___ be - lieve ___ that   we   might ___ last   a _____

thou -   sand _____ years   or   more ___ if   not ____ for ____

____ this?   Our _____ flesh   and _____ blood,   it ____ ties

End double-time feel

____ you   and   me ___ right   up. ___ Tie ____ me   down.   Oh, ___

Chorus

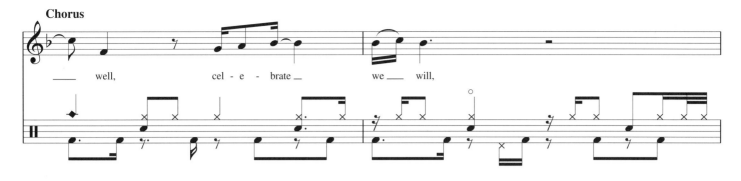

___ well, cel - e - brate ___ we ___ will,

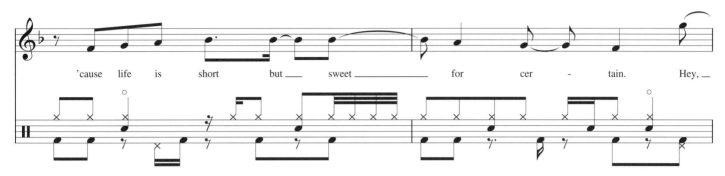

'cause life is short but ___ sweet _____ for cer - tain. Hey, ___

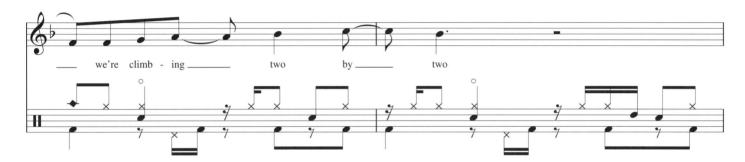

___ we're climb - ing _____ two by ___ two

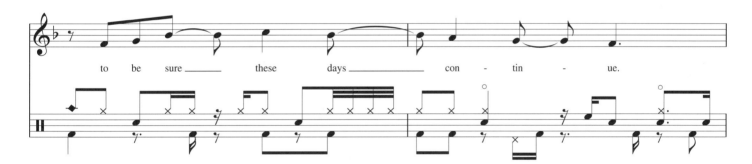

to be sure ____ these days _____ con - tin - ue.

Double-time feel

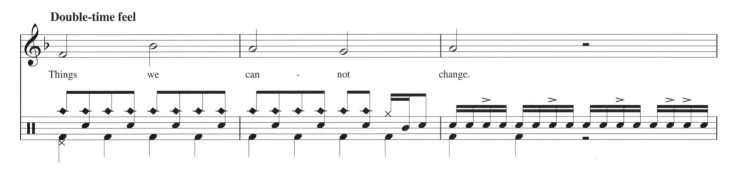

Things we can - not change.

Change.

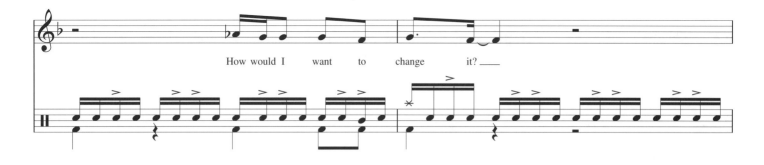

How would I want to change it? ____

Change. ____

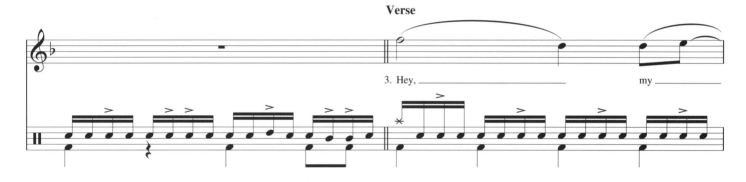

Verse

3. Hey, _____ my ____

w/ Drum Fig. 1 (8 times)

____ love, you came ____ to me like wine comes ____ to this ____

mouth, ____ grown ____ tired ____ of wa - ter all ____ the

time. You ____ quench ____ my ____ heart and, oh, ____

72

you _____ quench _____ my _____ mind. _____ And _____ say, _____

Chorus

_____ cel - e - brate _____ we _____ will,

'cause life is short but _____ sweet _____ for cer - tain. Hey, _____

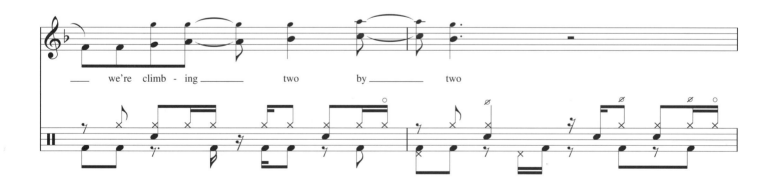

_____ we're climb - ing _____ two by _____ two

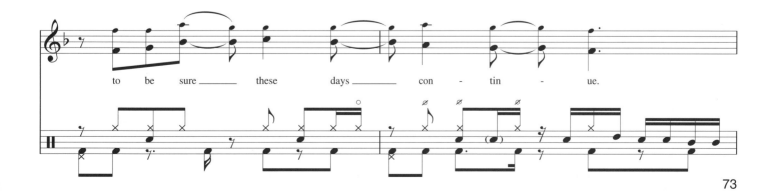

to be sure _____ these days _____ con - tin - ue.

73

Things   we   can...   I ____ must ____ cel - e -

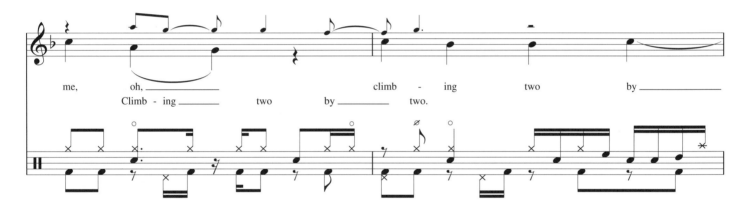

brate. _____   Yeah, oh, _____ you   and

(Cel - e - brate __ we   will.

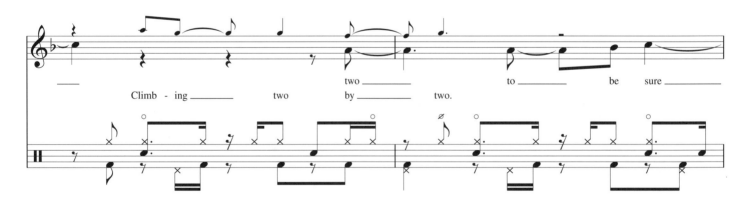

me,   oh, _____   climb - ing   two   by ____

Climb - ing ____ two   by ____ two.

two _____   to ____ be   sure ____

Climb - ing ____ two   by ____ two.

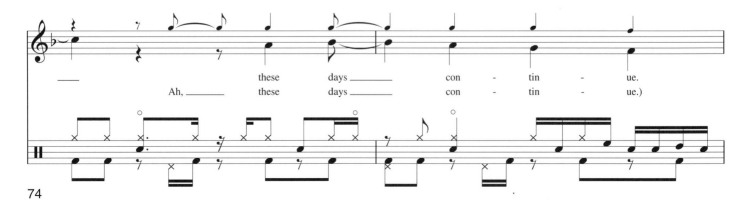

     these   days ____ con - tin - ue.

Ah, ____ these   days ____ con - tin - ue.)

Double-time feel

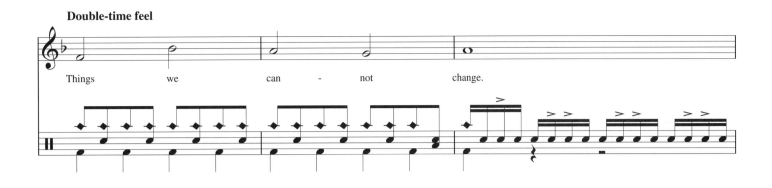

Things we can - not change.

Change.

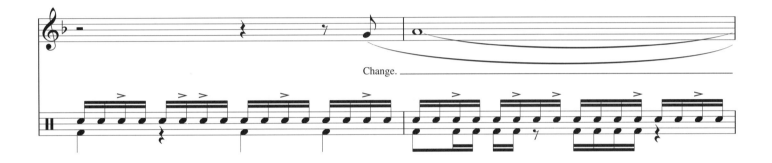

Change. _____

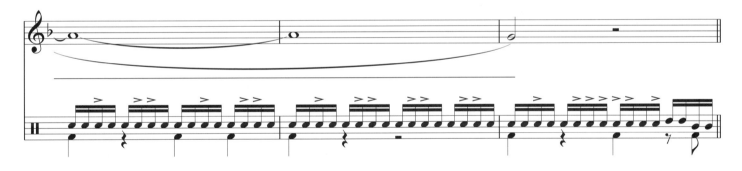

Verse

w/ Drum Fig. 1 (8 times)

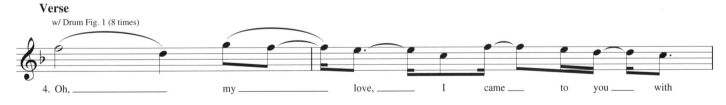

4. Oh, _____ my _____ love, _____ I came _____ to you _____ with

best in - ten - tions. _____ You _____ lay _____

_____ down and give _____ to me _____ just what I'm _____ seek - ing. _____

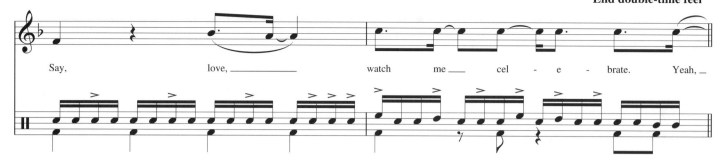

Say, love, _____ watch me _ cel - e - brate. Yeah, _

Chorus

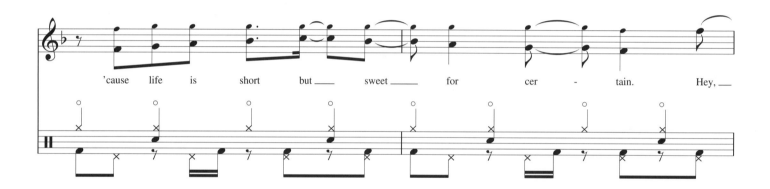

_____ oh, cel - e - brate _____ we ___ will,

'cause life is short but ___ sweet _____ for cer - tain. Hey, _

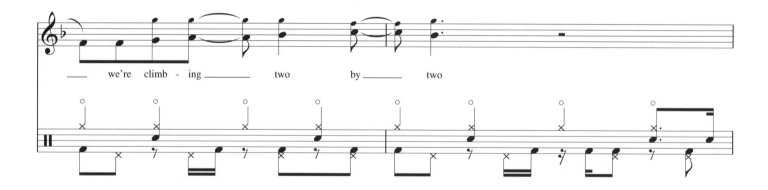

___ we're climb - ing _____ two by _____ two

Double-time feel

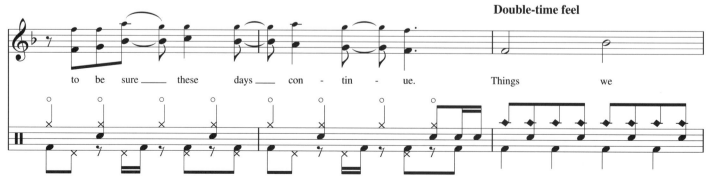

to be sure ___ these days ___ con - tin - ue. Things we

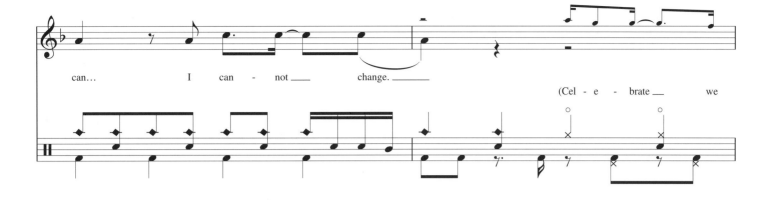

can…   I   can - not ____   change. ____

(Cel - e - brate ____ we

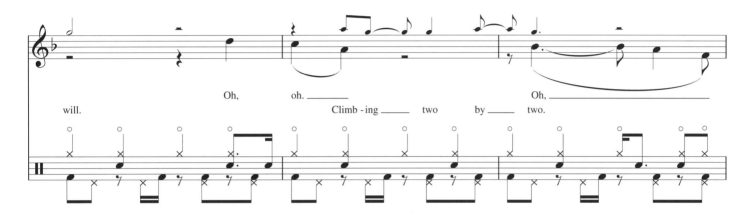

will.   Oh,   oh. ____   Climb - ing ____ two   by ____ two.   Oh, _____

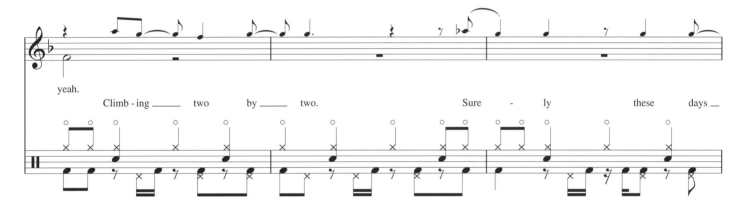

yeah.   Climb - ing ____ two   by ____ two.   Sure - ly   these   days ____

Double time feel

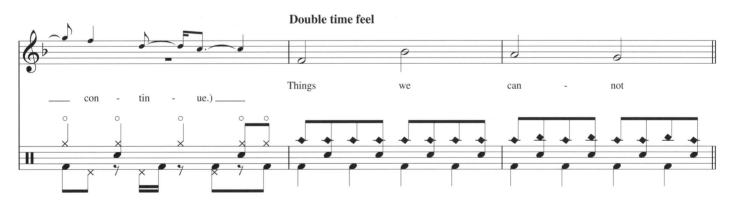

____ con - tin - ue.) ____   Things   we   can - not

Outro

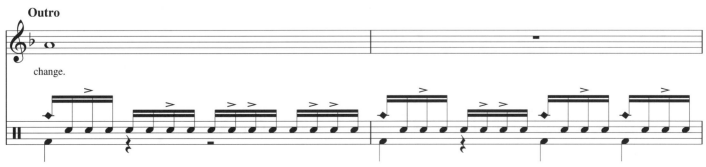

change.

w/ Voc. ad lib (till end)

Begin fade

Fade out

WAREHOUSE

Words and Music by
David J. Matthews

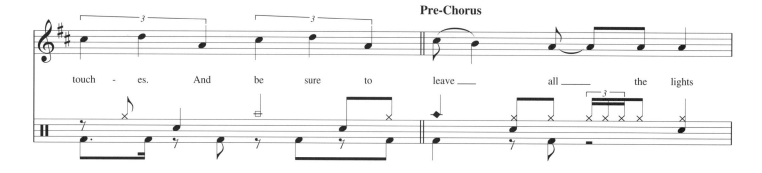

Pre-Chorus

touch - es. And be sure to leave all ___ the lights

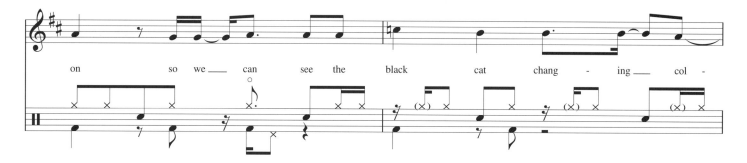

on so we ___ can see the black cat chang - ing ___ col -

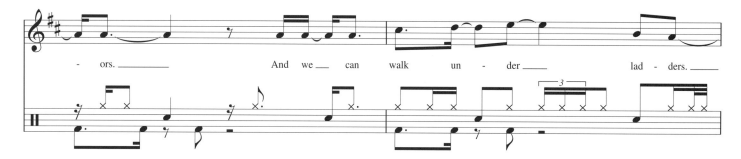

- ors. And we ___ can walk un - der ___ lad - ders. ___

And swim as ___ the ___ tide ___ turns ___ you a -

w/ Bkgd. Voc. Fig. 1

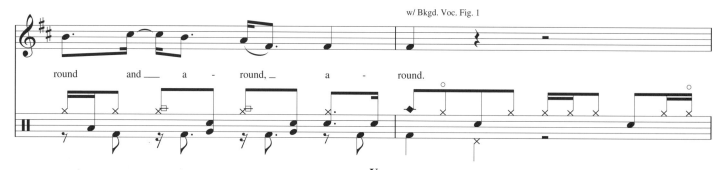

round and ___ a - round, ___ a - round.

Verse

w/ Bkgd. Voc. Fig. 1 (4 times)

3. Hey! We have ___ found, ___

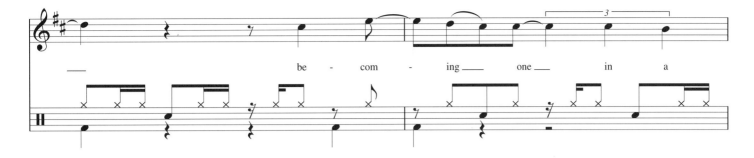

be - com - ing ___ one ___ in a

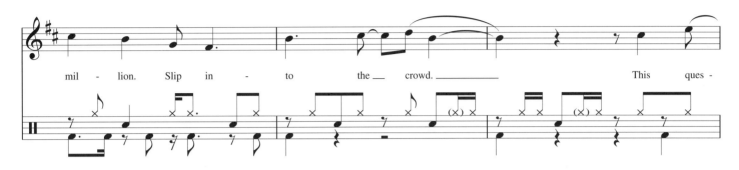

mil - lion. Slip in - to the ___ crowd. ___ This ques -

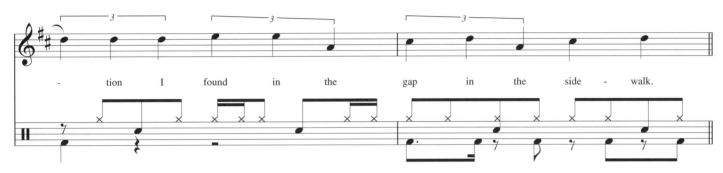

- tion I found in the gap in the side - walk.

Pre-Chorus

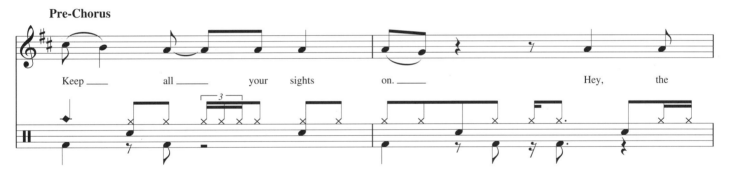

Keep ___ all ___ your sights on. ___ Hey, the

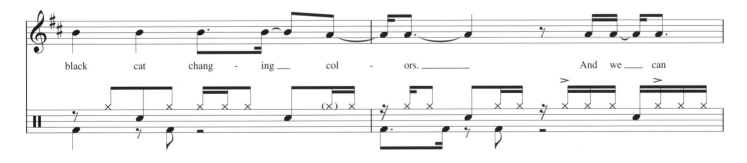

black cat chang - ing ___ col - ors. ___ And we ___ can

walk un - der ___ lad - ders. ___ And

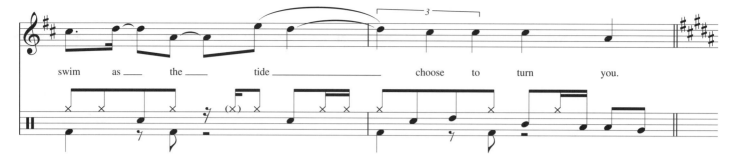

swim as the tide choose to turn you.

Chorus

And here I sit, life goes on. End of

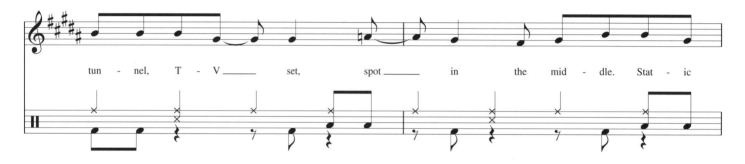

tun - nel, T - V set, spot in the mid - dle. Stat - ic

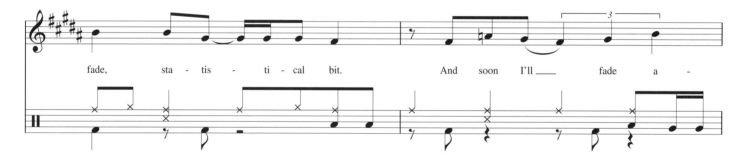

fade, sta - tis - ti - cal bit. And soon I'll fade a -

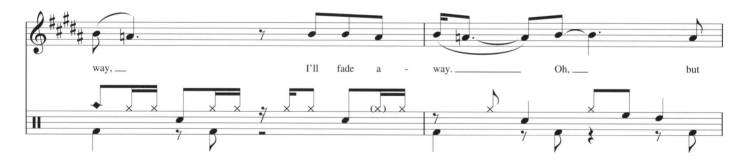

way, I'll fade a - way. Oh, but

this I ad - mit. Tastes so good, hard to be -

lieve an end to it.   Smell, _____ touch,   feel. _____ How could this

rhy - thm ev - er _____ quit?   Bags _____ packed _____ on a plane, _____

_   hope - ful - ly to   heav - en. _____ Well. _____

w/ Bkgd. Voc. Fig. 1 (2 times)

Verse

w/ Bkgd. Voc. Fig. 1 (4 times)

4. Shut   up!   I'm   think -   ing. _____   I   had _

_ a   clue, ____ now   it's   gone   for - ev -   er.   Sit - ting

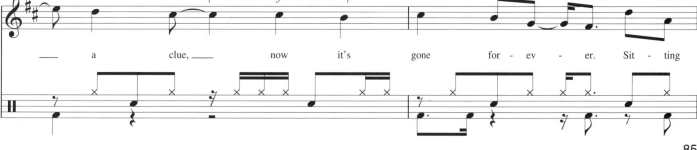

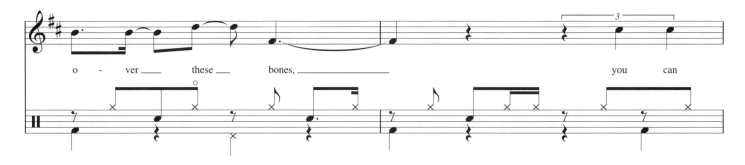

o - ver these bones, _____ you can

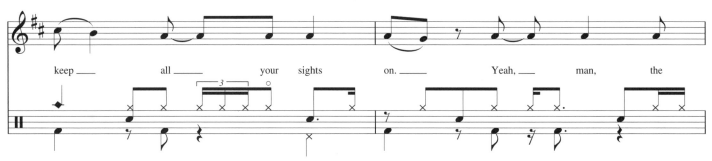

read in what - ev - er you're need - ing _____ to

Pre-Chorus

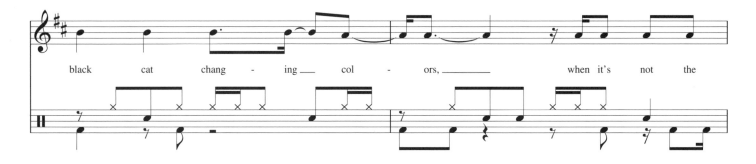

keep __ all __ your sights on. __ Yeah, __ man, the

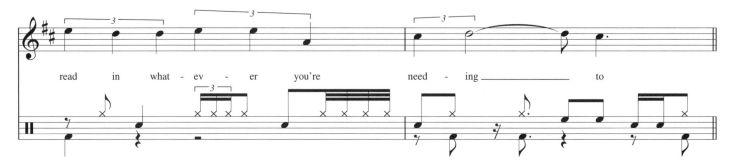

black cat chang - ing __ col - ors, _____ when it's not the

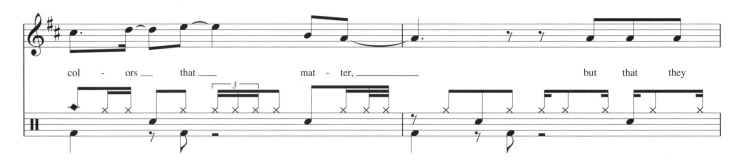

col - ors __ that __ mat - ter, _____ but that they

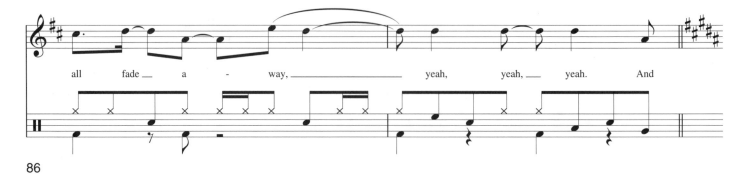

all fade __ a - way, _____ yeah, yeah, __ yeah. And

Chorus

I, _____ life ___ goes ___ on. End of tun - nel, T - V ___ set, spot _

___ in the mid - dle. Stat - ic fade, sta - tis - ti - cal bit. And soon I'll ___ fade a -

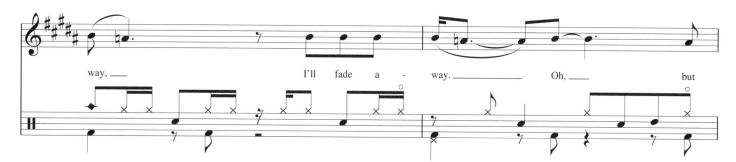

way, ___ I'll fade a - way. _____ Oh, ___ but

this I ___ ad - mit. Seems ___ so ___ good, hard to be -

lieve an end to it. The ware - house is bare, noth - ing it's

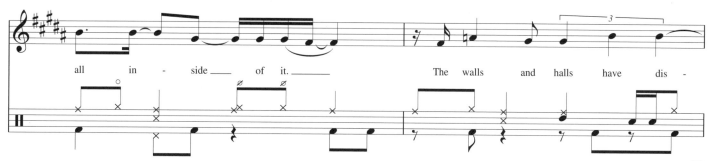

all in - side ___ of it. _____ The walls and halls have dis -

-ap - peared, _____ they've dis - ap - peared, _____ well. _____

My love, I'd love to stay here. _____

My love, I'd love to stay here. _____ My love, I'd

love to stay here. _____ My love, I'd love to stay here. _____

In a cor - ner, was won - d'ring if a change _____

could be bet - ter than this. Oh, _____ then I wor - ry

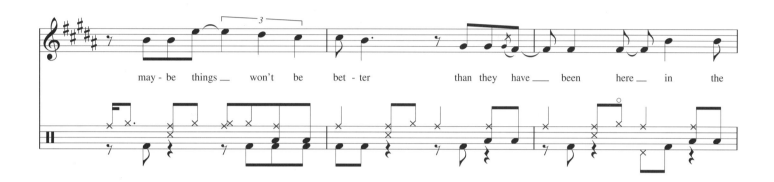

may - be things ___ won't be bet - ter _____ than they have ___ been here ___ in the

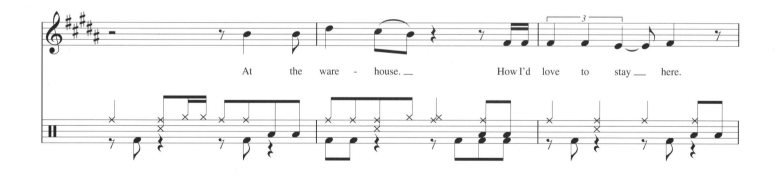

ware - house. ___ At the ware - house. ___

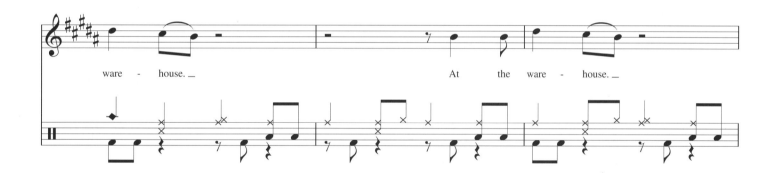

At the ware - house. ___ How I'd love to stay ___ here.

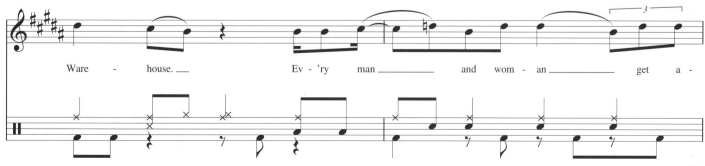

Ware - house. ___ Ev - 'ry man _____ and wom - an _____ get a -

live.

Ooh, __ that's our __

__ blood __ down there. __ It seems poured __ from __ the hands

of an - gels. __ But __ trick - le __ in - to the __ ground leaves the

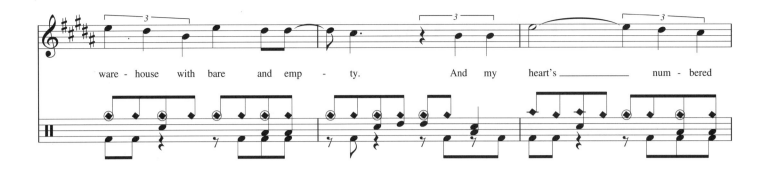

ware - house with bare and emp - ty. And my heart's _____ num - bered

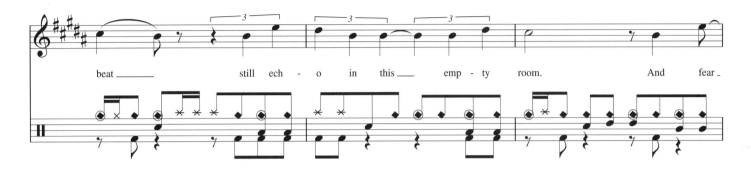

beat _____ still ech - o in this ___ emp - ty room. And fear ___

___ wells in ___ me. ___ But noth - ing seems good e - nough to ___

___ de - fend. I'll go a - way, _____ I'll a go a - way, ___

w/ Bkgd. Voc. Fig. 1

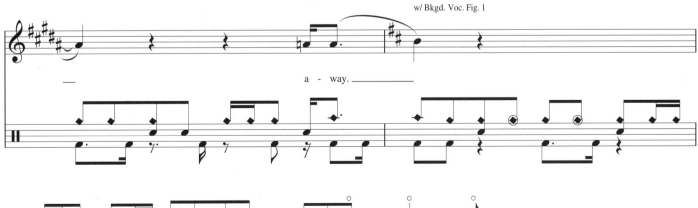

a - way. _____

rit.

WHERE ARE YOU GOING

Lyrics by David J. Matthews
Music by Dave Matthews Band

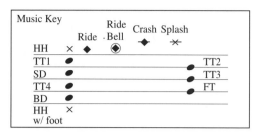

Intro

Moderately slow ♩ = 100

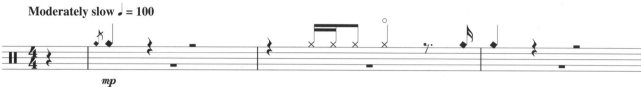

Verse

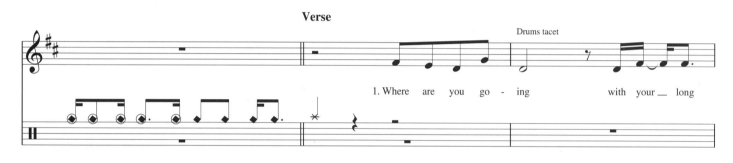

1. Where are you go - ing with your long face pull - ing down? Don't hide a - way like an o - cean, but you can't see but you can smell and the sound waves crash

*Soft mallets on crash w/ rivets.

Chorus

down. I am no Su - per - man, I have no rea - sons for you. I am no he - ro, oh, that's for sure.

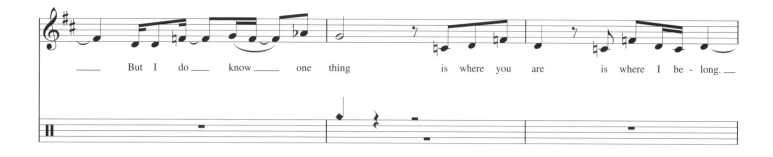

But I do __ know __ one thing is where you are is where I be - long. __

__ I do know where you go _____ is where I want to be. __

mf

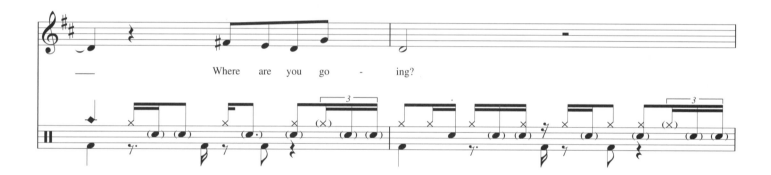

__ Where are you go - ing?

Where do you go? __

Verse

2. Are you look - ing for __ an - swers _____ to ques -

-tions _____ un - der the stars? Well, if a - long the way _____

_____ you are grow - ing wea - ry, you can rest with

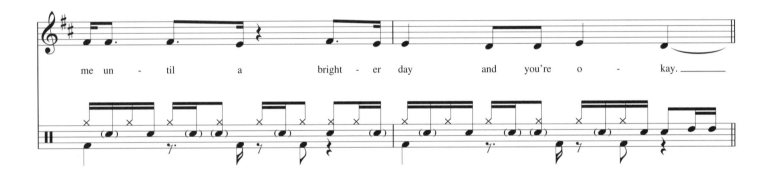

me un - til a bright - er day and you're o - kay. _____

Chorus

I am _____ no Su - per - man, _____

I have _____ no _____ an - swers _____ for you.

I am ___ no he - ro, ___ oh, ___ that's ___ for sure. ___

___ But I do ___ know ___ one thing ___ is where you

are ___ is where I be - long. ___ I do

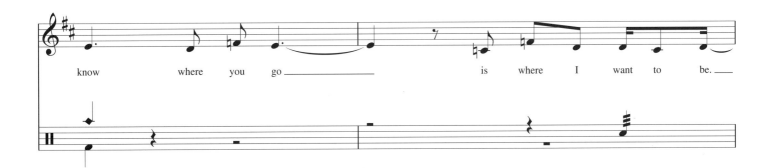

know where you go ___ is where I want to be. ___

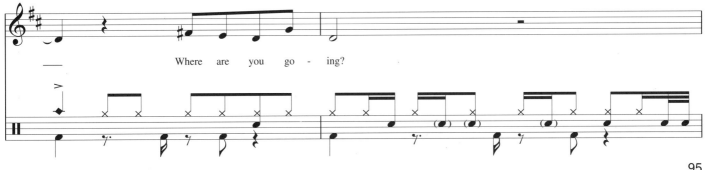

___ Where are you go - ing?

Where do you go? _

Interlude

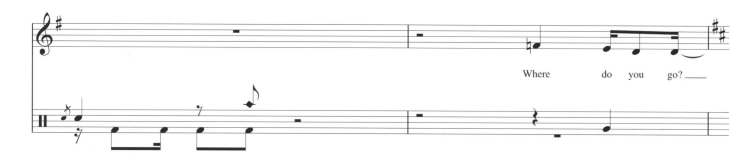

Where do you go? _____

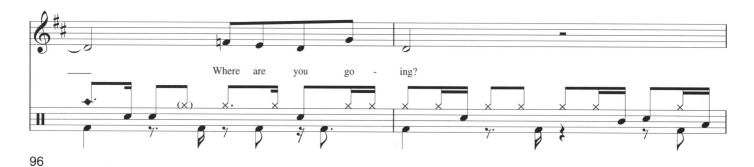

Where are you go - ing?

Where do you go? —

Chorus

— I am — no Su-per-man, —

I have — no — an - swers — for you. —

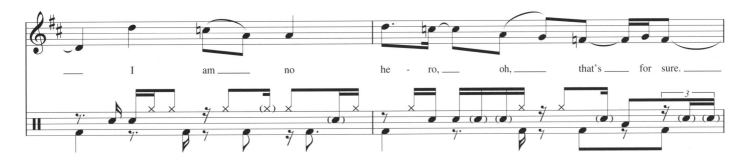

— I am — no he-ro, — oh, — that's — for sure. —

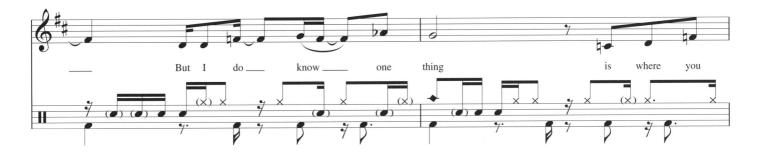

— But I do — know — one thing — is where you

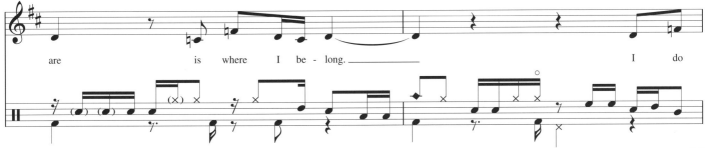

are — is where I be-long. — I do

know where you go _____ is where I want to be. ___ Where are you go -

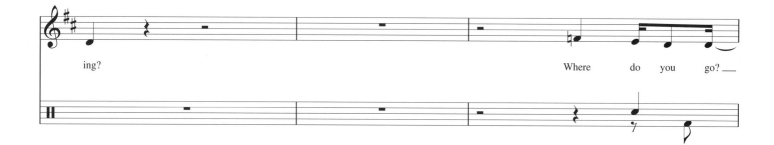

ing? Where do you go? ___

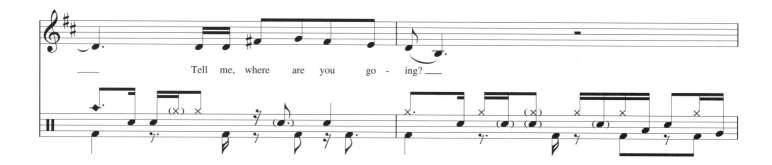

___ Tell me, where are you go - ing? ___

Where... _____

Outro

Yeah, ___ let's go. ___

HI-HAT

OPEN AND CLOSED HI-HAT: Strike the open hi-hat on notes labeled with an *o.* Strike the closed hi-hat on unlabeled notes.

HI-HAT WITH FOOT: Clap hi-hat cymbals together with foot pedal.

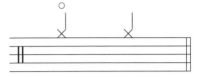

HI-HAT WITH SLUR: The open hi-hat is struck and then closed with the foot on the beat indicated by the hi-hat w/foot notation below, creating a *shoop* sound.

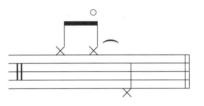

HI-HAT BARK: The open hi-hat is struck and is immediately, almost simultaneously closed so that the *shoop* sound is severely clipped.

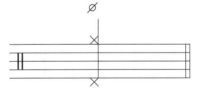

CYMBALS

CHOKE: Hit the crash cymbal and catch it immediately with the other hand, producing a short, choked crash sound.

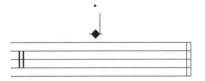

BELL OF CYMBAL: Hit the cymbal near the center, directly on the cup or bell portion.

CYMBAL ROLL: Play a roll on the cymbal rapidly enough to produce a sustained, uninterrupted *shhh* sound lasting for the number of beats indicated.

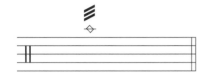

DRUMS

CROSS STICK: Anchor the tip end of the stick on the snare drum skin at the eight o'clock position, two to three inches from the rim. Then raise and lower the butt end, striking the rim at the two o'clock position, producing a clicky, woodblock-type sound.

FLAM: Hit the drum with both sticks, one slightly after the other, producing a single, thick-sounding note.

RUFF: Play the grace notes rapidly and as close to the principal note as possible. The grace notes are unaccented and should be played slightly before the beat. The principal note is accented and played directly on the beat.

CLOSED ROLL: Play a roll on the snare drum creating a sustained, uninterrupted *tshhh* sound lasting for the duration of the rhythm indicated and with no break between the two tied notes.

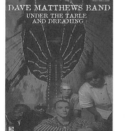